Slaves among Us

Slaves among Us

The Hidden World
of Human Trafficking

MONIQUE VILLA

ROWMAN & LITTLEFIELD
Lanham • Boulder • New York • London

Published by Rowman & Littlefield
An imprint of The Rowman & Littlefield Publishing Group, Inc.
4501 Forbes Boulevard, Suite 200, Lanham, Maryland 20706
www.rowman.com

6 Tinworth Street, London SE11 5AL, United Kingdom

Distributed by NATIONAL BOOK NETWORK

British Library Cataloguing in Publication Information Available

Library of Congress Cataloging-in-Publication Data

Names: Villa, Monique, author.
Title: Slaves among us : the hidden world of human trafficking / Monique Villa.
Description: Lanham : Rowman & Littlefield, [2019] | Includes index.
Identifiers: LCCN 2019000255 (print) | LCCN 2019003562 (ebook) | ISBN
    9781538127292 (electronic) | ISBN 9781538127285 (cloth : alk. paper)
Subjects: LCSH: Slavery—History—21st century.
Classification: LCC HT867 (ebook) | LCC HT867 .V55 2019 (print) | DDC
    306.3/6209/05—dc23
LC record available at https://lccn.loc.gov/2019000255

To the survivors I had the privilege to meet in the
last ten years and to the millions I don't know.
And to Chloe, Baptiste, Charlotte, Celeste, and Pia.

Those who have the privilege to know have the duty to act.

—*Albert Einstein*

Contents

Acknowledgments

I could not have written this book without the remarkable survivors who trusted me enough to open their lives to me, even in their most difficult circumstances. They were my heroes before writing this book and they still are people I think of on a daily basis—even Jennifer Kempton, whose courage and lucidity will go a long way to make us all understand how one can fall prey to traffickers.

The reason why I started this book was the pressing need I felt to shed light on this abominable crime; I wanted to make it easy to understand and to raise awareness so that fewer innocent people become victims. I hope it will reach a young public.

I could not have written this book without the fantastic help of Wylie O'Sullivan, who was my attentive, sensitive, and very demanding editor.

I also want to thank my fantastic team at the Thomson Reuters Foundation and especially Antonio Zappulla, my number two, for their unwavering support.

And of course, I am deeply grateful to the many specialists on the issue who spent so much time answering my questions and explaining to me obscure aspects of the trade that I found difficult to understand—in no particular order: Kevin Bales, Cornelius Katona, Evelyn Chumbow, Cyrus Vance, Kailash Satyarthi, Sumedha Satyarthi, Alpana Rawat, David

Batstone, Martina Vandenberg, Kevin Hyland, Ben Skinner, Jessica Graham, Mary Fisher, Barry Koch, Aditi Wanchoo, Giles Bolton, Nick Grono, Karen Friedman Agnifilo, Carolina Holderness, Manan Ansari, Minh Dang, Chen Guangcheng, Ajeet Singh, Sunita Danuwar, and Cecilia Flores-Oebanda—and, of course, Anish Kapoor, for his passionate and long-lasting support.

I worked on this book during my holidays and weekends in 2017 and the first half of 2018, and I had the extraordinary privilege to be a resident at the Rockefeller Foundation villa in Bellagio to finish it in ideal conditions. My heartfelt thanks go to Pilar Palacia and her team—and to Raj Shah, for keeping this place like a paradise for authors and all kinds of academics and artists.

Preface: Why?

We were having dinner at Bond 45 in Manhattan with my friend and Reuters colleague Saidah, who adores Paris, and I was telling her that I am a rare specimen of a real Parisian, born from generations of Parisians on my mother's side. "Lucky you," she said. "I have no idea where my family comes from. We were slaves. I don't know where my ancestors were living before they reached America."

This was my first contact with the reality of slavery. It was twelve years ago, and I still remember that moment vividly. Thanks to my colleague, I suddenly realized that most of my black American friends were probably in the same situation as Saidah. For a tenth-generation Parisian, it came as a shock.

I found it extraordinary that 150 years after the abolition of slavery in the United States, the wounds were still so deep under the skin: in a way, Saidah was still looking for her identity.

On November 4, 2008, I was with her again, this time in Harlem, to experience a joyful and truly historic night: the election of the first black president of the United States, Barack Obama, whose wife Michelle was also a descendant of slaves. By that time, I had started to get interested in modern-day slavery, because it does indeed exist around the world—merely camouflaged in different costumes.

I had just been appointed CEO of the Thomson Reuters Foundation. Earlier that year, Reuters had been acquired by Thomson. Tom Glocer, the CEO, asked me to take the Reuters Foundation and transform it into a bigger Thomson Reuters Foundation that would have greater impact and give a culture to the new corporation. He chose me for the job, he said later, because "if you have a big company and a relatively small foundation, you want something that can push above its weight, and someone who barges into the CEO's office and says: 'We must do this!'" He had no difficulty in convincing me to take the job.

My brief was challenging, and I started to think about how and where we could have maximum impact. The big question was how the skills of the company could help drive social progress for the voiceless and the forgotten. I trusted my instinct and saw incredible potential for action— collective action. I started to think about the atrocity of modern-day slavery and how to effect change in its pernicious world. Since childhood, I have been driven by curiosity and the need to understand what is hiding behind the power of the people in power. That's why I chose to be a journalist, with a life that drove me to live in Rome, London, and Paris, covering all kinds of stories, from politics to diplomatic crises and even the divorce of Charles and Diana.

I have always trusted my gut feelings, ever since I almost died at twenty-two, when I spent three days in a deep coma, intubated, after a particularly nasty asthma attack. Waking in the reanimation room of the Laennec Hospital in Paris, I realized two things that completely changed my life.

First and above all, I was devastated that I could have died without having achieved anything of merit. This gave me a sense of urgency that has never left me: I'd better hurry to do a few good things, as I knew now that life could be very short.

Second, I felt, almost to the point of certitude, that God didn't exist. At the time, reading was a passion. I had read *War and Peace* multiple times and *The Leopard* twice. In both books, the main characters die. In the moments before their deaths, both see a flashback of their lives and a great light that brings a sense of peace. That always seemed to me like a metaphor for catching a glimpse of God.

But during my severe asthma attack, I had seen nothing—no light, no God—nothing but a desperate search for my breath. As I could not breathe, death would have come as a relief, an end to suffocating, final peace for an exhausted body. But I had survived, with a rage to do something with my life, and I strongly believed in my freedom to choose what I wanted to do, refusing all kinds of dogma.

Freedom. I think this is what led me to believe that the new foundation I was called to lead should help those who were completely deprived of freedom. Almost by accident, I started to meet people who were deeply involved in the fight against human trafficking and modern slavery.

At the time, ten years ago, I knew very little about what it means to be a slave in the twenty-first century. And I certainly had no clue how you could turn a human being into a commodity. The idea that children, men, and women could be exploited, beaten, tortured, sold, resold, and forced into total submission—and then discarded when they are no longer useful—was revolting to me. I had no clear understanding of how slaves could escape or of the complicated details behind rescue operations.

I started this journey into this unknown world driven by a profound curiosity—the same curiosity that led me into journalism years ago. In fact, my approach was identical. I learned by speaking to those with knowledge. I reached out to the NGOs fighting slavery on the front lines, to the lawyers working pro bono to help victims get compensation for their years of unpaid work, to the academics studying the issue globally, to government officials in a few countries, to police forces and prosecutors, and of course, to investigative journalists who spoke my language.

But it was through the survivors that I really grew to understand the huge scope and the particularities of such global crime. Some of them have become my heroes, and I want this book to tell their stories and show their courage, because I am convinced that knowledge triggers action.

My hope is that through this book, more people will become aware of modern slavery. It is an invisible crime, but once it has been pointed out, it's easier to take notice. And once we take notice, with the right knowledge we can take action. As consumers, for instance, we have a choice and a voice. We can avoid buying at least some of the goods tainted by forced labor. As Einstein said, "Those who have the privilege to know have the duty to act."

I feel that my contribution to ending the scourge of modern slavery is essentially connecting the dots: joining all the different experts, legislators, lawyers, CEOs, and people taking action on the ground to bring about real change for the millions who are suffering as you read this book. I try to bring together as many people as possible and break down the silos in which they work separately. Together, we take action. I try to make survivors feel that they are respected as extraordinary human beings, stronger than most. They are central in the fight against slavery: not only do they have the necessary knowledge and the experience, but they are also the ones to whom other vulnerable people will listen.

And most of us can help, if we choose to see. A number of positive things have started to happen in the last five years, and many different types of solutions have emerged. Each of us can play a role in the fight: as consumers, as citizens, and as human beings. This book offers an opportunity to explore how.

Slavery has existed since the beginning of human history, yet this does not mean that it's inevitable. If we take collective action, we will change the course of history and bring it to an end.

My first tangible memory of taking action as an individual is linked to the Trust Women Conference (now called the Trust Conference), an event that I conceived and launched in 2012 to shed light on modern slavery and to put the rule of law behind women's rights.

It was at our second conference, on a cold day in December 2013 in the city of London. A Nepalese man, Deependra, had just explained to the audience how he had been lured into slavery through the promise of an office job in Qatar. Once he arrived in Doha, his passport was taken away from him, and Deependra found himself forced to work in terrible conditions without the freedom to leave. He was lucky—he finally managed to escape after two-and-a-half years.

At the time we met, Deependra was still working in another Emirate state, no longer as a slave but at a low wage, to repay his debt. He had no idea how long it would take him to repay the loan he had taken to pay the recruiter who organized his "job" in Qatar and his flight from Kathmandu. The interest rate on the loan was 60 percent. This is what is called "bonded labor," or "debt bondage." It happens to people trapped both in forced labor and in sexual slavery. Millions of people around the world have lost their freedom to bonded labor. Some even inherit bonded labor at birth because their parents have been unable to pay off their debt.

The panel on which Deependra was speaking had just finished when someone in the room, whom I had never met before—a tall, soft-spoken, polite, and elegant lady in her early sixties—came up to me and said she wanted to settle his debt on his behalf. "Do you think he would accept my offer?" We will call her M as she doesn't want publicity.

I spoke to Deependra, and he was of course delighted to meet her. We walked into a small room. And there I witnessed the biggest act of generosity I had ever seen: a stranger changing the course of the life of another stranger and his entire family.

M asked him, "How much is your debt?"

"Four thousand dollars," Deependra replied. For him, this was a huge sum that would have taken years to repay, especially with interest accumulating all the time. But for most of the conference attendees, $4,000 was in fact a relatively modest sum that many of us could have helped him repay.

"I will give you $10,000 and you can use that money to go back to your family and start your own business in Nepal," said M.

Deependra was overjoyed and said his dream was to create his own charity to help other Nepalese men and women avoid falling prey to traffickers.

For the first time, I felt I had contributed to improving the life of a victim of the worst of all human crimes. I was so happy that, thanks to M's generosity, we could radically transform Deependra's life. I immediately had his return plane ticket changed. Two days later, he flew back to Kathmandu to meet his wife and daughter as a free man.

One fact that has struck me more and more throughout the years is that in order to be a trafficker, you need to see the person you enslave as a thing or as an animal, not as a human being, so that you can torture them without remorse.

Anti-trafficking work is a robust refusal of this dehumanization; enslaved people are as human as we are, with the same needs, fears, and hopes. In this book, I'll tell the stories of three extraordinary people who survived slavery: Jennifer Kempton, Deependra Giri, and Marcela Loaiza. They show what can happen to you when you are at your most vulnerable. All three escaped slavery, but none of them saw their traffickers prosecuted or put in jail.

"These are just three women I help," says one trafficker in this book. Three women that he controls, abuses, and dehumanizes. And doesn't help.

1

Who Are the Modern Slaves?

So who are the modern slaves? They are not chained as they were in the past. They can walk among us. For example, we can end up tipping one at a respectable hotel without knowing his or her circumstances; we wear dresses and accessories one has made; we can even be seated on a plane next to one. They look like us, although they inhabit a totally different universe.

The definition accepted by the best experts is that a slave is someone who is forced to work, through fraud or threat of violence, for no pay beyond subsistence. The biggest difference between ancient slavery and its modern form is that the former was almost always for life, whereas now slaves are more likely to be trapped for a few years, or even a few months, before being thrown away. In this era of mass consumption, slaves are only as good and valuable as their abilities. Once they are no longer useful—for example, if they have become ill or injured while working—they are discarded and abandoned to a twilight zone that can be as cruel and damaging as slavery itself.

Slavery is a flourishing global business today. Never in the history of human beings have there been so many slaves. Estimates vary, but there could be more than one hundred million adults and children enslaved across the world today. It is a vast, hidden, and perpetually evolving horror, and it is a difficult area on which to gather definitive data.

In 2017, conservative statistics from the International Labor Organization (ILO) and the Walk Free Foundation put the number at 40.3 million slaves worldwide. If slavery were a country or a state, it would have the population of Algeria or California. This figure of 40.3 million is based on available data, but most experts agree that the number is actually far higher. Unfortunately, in the absence of better information, it is the best we have at this point, and it is at least closer to the truth than the ILO's previous estimate of 20.9 million. But the lack of accurate data is a real and ongoing challenge when it comes to tackling the problem.

The best specialists estimate that 30 percent of slaves are trafficked for sex and 70 percent are in forced labor, though of course the ratio varies from country to country. So far, forced labor remains even less visible that sex trafficking, which has in recent years received media and government attention. Prosecutors are increasingly pursuing sex-trafficking cases in some countries, whereas they have a much harder time bringing forced-labor cases to court.

A big part of the problem is that people simply don't understand forced labor—that it exists in the supply chains of many of the brands we buy and in the service industries such as car washes, nail salons, and hotels, in every country. Prosecutors have to prove that traffickers have used fraud, coercion, or the threat of violence to induce someone to work and that they are not paying the person above subsistence.

This is why prosecutors often find it easier to pursue traffickers for money laundering or tax fraud than for trafficking. As the penalties are more or less the same, they go for the easier offense. The problem is that this approach doesn't help assemble reliable data.

Getting the figures right is crucial—so that governments, corporations, the media, and the general public understand the true scope of this horror and where and how to combat it. Accurate data would also allow us to determine if we are making progress or if things are getting worse.

Kailash Satyarthi, the Peace Nobel Prize laureate who has saved thousands of children from slavery in India and runs two ashrams where he looks after survivors, recently told me that he believes there could be as many as 30 million children enslaved in India today—dramatically higher than official estimates. His team thinks the number could be even greater. If that is the number of children forced to work as slaves in India, imagine the number of adults trapped in the same condition. With a population of 1.3 billion people, the country is home to the largest number of enslaved people, followed by China.

Unfortunately, slavery can flourish easily because circumstances favor the exploiters and work against the victims. Slavery is an invisible and silent crime.

Slaves cannot shout for help because they are abused, beaten, and sometimes tortured into submission. I have seen more survivors than I can count scarred by cigarette burns and other unspeakable forms of branding. I'll never forget the fifteen-year-old Indian boy at Kailash's ashram who told me that in the New Delhi sweatshop where he was exploited, his master's favorite form of punishment was to fasten a child to a fan and watch it spin him around to guarantee that he remained obedient. The cruelty deployed to keep people in that state is unimaginable.

Very often, slaves don't even know that they have been enslaved. All the children I spoke to during my visit to Kailash's ashram in Rajasthan in May 2017 had believed that their parents were being paid for their work and that they were helping their families survive. It was not the case.

If they are fortunate enough to escape the hell of slavery, survivors risk finding themselves in another kind of hell. After years of abuse, they have lost their dignity, their self-respect, and their ability to trust anybody. They are incredibly vulnerable and the risk is that they will soon be re-trafficked if they don't receive adequate help. Starting a new life beyond slavery is challenging, even if the enslavement has been for a relatively short period. Many survivors can only start to find comfort when they spend time with other former slaves. These are the people they can relate to and begin to trust.

The road to full freedom is a very long and painful one, and much psychological work is required to try to rebuild so many shattered souls. Unfortunately, there are not many psychologists around the world who understand the very particular needs of survivors. Those who do have experience treating human-trafficking victims explain that survivors continue to be vulnerable to exactly the same things that have happened to them before.

Cornelius Katona, a psychiatrist at the Helen Bamber Foundation in London, who specializes in survivors coming from Eastern Europe, explains, "Just as for domestic violence, they feel that what has happened is what they deserved or is inevitable. So they lose their self-esteem, their self-worth; they lose the ability to forgive themselves, to feel compassionate about themselves. They have to learn compassion, and we do that in group therapy: if other people show you compassion, it becomes a little easier to have compassion for yourself and feel less guilty."

Kailash Satyarthi told me once that two children he had recently rescued were unable to interact with the other kids at the ashram. They would sit at the edge of the group in silence, even after being there for two weeks. One of them eventually asked another child, "Why are these people so kind to us? Do they want our eyes or our kidneys?" They could simply not imagine the very concept of kindness.

We must help the survivors of slavery: they need therapy, many need addiction treatments, most of them need the education they have been denied, and they need lawyers who can fight for their rights and for redress. We need survivors' networks in every country because slavery is everywhere: in the United States, in the United Kingdom, in France and Italy, as well as in Africa and all over Asia.

But survivors are not victims. In my view, they are among the strongest of human beings: they have survived hell on earth and the abuse of those who have enslaved them, yet they have found the mental energy to resist and escape. Survivors are incredibly resilient and adaptable, qualities that can help them rebuild their lives. Of course, like anyone else, they need a little bit of luck and help.

Many victims are seduced into slavery with a simple sentence: "Would you like a job?" Kevin Bales, professor of contemporary slavery at the University of Nottingham, who has written extensively about modern slavery and is one of the world's top specialists, says that to anyone living in poverty and desperate to provide for themselves and their families, these are magic words. They are ready to take any job, at any cost.

Slavery afflicts both men and women, but the nature of women's bodies means that there is extra scope to exploit them. Women may be forced to surrender their wombs if their masters make them pregnant. The child might then be sold, disposed of, manipulated, or broken up into "human components" that can be sold to feed all kind of organs traffic, as Kevin Bales explains. Children are also a way for traffickers to keep the woman under their control because they will need the father's support.

Forced labor and sex trafficking have a great deal in common and those subjected to either one feel a total sense of betrayal and helplessness. Just as in sex trafficking, many people in forced labor are raped in order to be subjugated: on fishing boats in Thailand, for example, where men have to fish for months on end, rape is a common feature.

The profits made through slavery are gigantic. The ILO puts the annual figure at $150 billion, but many specialists think it's probably closer to a trillion. It's an incredibly profitable business model, with very few risks attached. Slaveholders can discard their slaves and find new ones when their existing "commodities" become too ill or exhausted to yield further profits, because the price of a slave is so low today. The average price is $90, whereas the cost of a slave in the United States in the nineteenth century was the equivalent of $40,000 of today, according to historians.

This is organized crime at its best, driven by the traffickers' almost total impunity because prosecutions are so rare. In 2016, only 9,071 convictions were recorded worldwide. Low risks, high returns: this is the perfect recipe for a flourishing business.

2

The Most Despicable Crime
Techniques of the Human-Trafficking Business Model

I met Jennifer Kempton in person in April 2017, after a few long phone conversations across the ocean over the previous two years. At thirty-five, she was a beautiful woman in a kind of unpolished way: pale skin, untidy auburn hair, a delicate mouth with no sign of bitterness, a profound gaze, and an athletic, ivory body in a gym outfit. Her manners were very direct, but also very sweet. She had an enormous flower tattooed on the right side of her neck.

Her story was incredibly moving, but what struck me most were her strength and her intelligence. I had no doubt that it was this combination of traits that had enabled her to survive six years of enslavement, beatings, rapes, cigarette burns, tattoos of her slavers' names on different parts of her body, and an addiction to crack and heroin. Those same traits enabled her, eventually, to escape.

Less than one year after she got free, she had already created her own NGO, Survivor's Ink, to help other former slaves, even while she herself was still suffering tremendously from her trauma. She always seemed to think of others before herself.

We were in Washington, DC, for the Trust Conference in April 2017, where Jennifer participated in a panel. She dominated the conversation, and she was fantastic: her passion and clarity immediately won the audience's attention, respect, and goodwill. She reached into everyone's heart.

I was really impressed by Jennifer—by the way she expressed herself, her completely lucid analysis of what had happened to her, all the painful work of recovery she had undertaken, how much she had helped other survivors, everything she envisioned for the future. Her charitable organization had rapidly expanded in size and scope.

And it had only been four years since she'd escaped her traffickers! It was clear to me that she was going to build much bigger things.

The day we sat down together, we spoke for four hours. Jennifer had decided to tell it all, in the hope that her story would help others stay safe from traffickers.

I'll let her speak now in her own words:

Technically I was not trafficked until I was twenty-five years old. But in my opinion, it started with the molestation as an infant, the child abuse, the rape at the age of twelve.

That constant horror, the constant lack of support, the unaddressed trauma that just continued to add up to the point when my vulnerabilities were so extensive that my boyfriend was able to enslave me.

I met Salem after a breakup with my child's father. He just came into my life and treated me like a queen. Not so much financially, more emotionally. The "I love you," the "You are my everything," the "I want to be with you forever," and "I'd never hurt you" were just what I was craving. After being in a violent domestic relationship, and all the trauma and abuse in my life, I really clung on to that. And he got me highly dependent on him to fill these emotional voids I had.

My grooming process was probably nine months to a year. We dated for several months, then he moved me to his house for several months. My child and I lived with him. He provided everything for us.

During that period, he got me addicted to heroin and other heavy drugs. I was already using cocaine and marijuana when I met him, so it wasn't that difficult to transition. When he introduced the other drugs into the equation, I was terrified, but these were the drugs he did, and I loved him and wanted to be accepted. I wanted to be a part of whatever he was a part of. He was doing heroin even before I came into the picture, but I didn't know it. He hid it for a long time.

After he stuck me in the arm with a needle, he came to me a couple of days later and said, "Look, you have to choose one or the other—your drugs that you've always had, or this drug." And I felt like he was saying: Do you want to come with me? And I chose the scary, ridiculous drug because I felt like I was choosing him. I wanted to keep him.

A few months after, he came to me and said: "I love you so much and I'm so scared. We are losing everything. We are losing the house. I don't know what to do. You know, I have been taking care of you and your child. You want to be with me, right? You do really love me, right? Why don't you step up and take care of us now?'

It was all glitter, rainbows, wonderful feelings up until that point, and then it changed dramatically. I sent my child to live with my mom. His idea of me providing started with strip clubs.

I had to make enough money for the drugs for both of us, and for the hotel stay for the evening; we had to leave the house. If I didn't bring enough, he would pull away from me emotionally, not giving me the physical or verbal attention that I so deeply, intimately craved. He would pull the drugs away from me and leave me dope sick.

His mother didn't live too far away, and he would go over there and spend the night with her. And there were nights when I had to sleep in a cardboard box outside because I did not have enough money to cover everything he wanted plus a hotel. For several months, I strove to make the most money I could. The more money I made, the more attention I had from him. I was still very much in love with him.

I see the emotional manipulation now. I did not see it then. I was blind to the fact that this man fed me this dream of the perfect relationship that I so intensely desired. And then he just totally switched and started exploiting me, and I didn't even realize it. But I wasn't getting physically beaten at that point.

So, I was striving to make the most money I could make, but I was just not bringing enough for him. He approached me with another female. This woman had an addiction as well, but she had a house, she had a car, she was always going shopping. So, she was doing something "right," I thought.

They approached me together and they glamorized the idea of massage ads on Craigslist. They said, "It's just massage, you put on some sexy bra and panties and you make a little extra money. But other than that, you are just giving a legitimate massage. Instead of dancing in stilettos all night and maybe bringing two, three hundred dollars, you can make three, four, five, six, seven hundred dollars an hour."

For me that meant not only that I would have way more money to give the boyfriend for our drug habit, but also it would make the boyfriend happier. He would love me more. And I would have more time to spend with him. Also, this woman was going to give us a place to live. No more bouncing around. So, she moved us in, and for a couple of weeks she provided our drugs, our room and board, clothing—whatever we wanted and needed.

Then it came time to place the massage ad. She took pictures and told me, "If you wear this and you pose like this, and you give a sexy look, you are going to make more money. And I'm going to post the ad because I know the language to use. I'm going to answer the phone, too, because I need to screen those guys. I need to make sure that you're going to be safe, that you don't get any perverts or weirdos. I'm going to take care of you and make sure you are okay."

And since she'd been taking care of us, in my mind this was the solution to the issue I had been struggling with. So she placed the ad, and she took me in her car to my first client and informed me on the way there, "Oh, by the way, this is what you have to do to get my money." Wait, your money? "Yes, you owe me for everything I have done for you both in the last two weeks. And I am going to be sitting here in the car waiting for you and you better come back with my money. By the way, this guy, I've seen him before, he is a client of mine, so don't try any funny shit."

I really didn't feel I had much choice. Not only was I dependent on the drugs, I was dependent on the boyfriend, and, also, I had no insurance. There's a lack of resources available for people who don't have insurance and are opiate dependent and needing to go to a detox facility. There's nothing available. I couldn't have gone to get help if I wanted to. And what else was I going to do? My family—I had been isolated so deeply from them that they probably wouldn't have even taken a phone call from me. I didn't have anybody.

So, this chick is waiting in the car for me, I owe her money, and I didn't know what would happen if I didn't pay her. And this guy, she knows him, so I can't just call the police. I really felt like I had no other choice at that point in time. Or I had no cognitive ability to make a choice in that situation. I just swallowed my own vomit and went on my first strike. And he didn't give her the right amount of money, so she got mad and she put the two of us out of her house.

And the boyfriend took me to the west side of Columbus, and that's when I had to start jumping in and out of cars. I was making a third to a tenth of the money I could have made as an escort. I had to work that much more. That was when the crack cocaine was introduced into the equation. Because I had that much money to make and I had to stay awake and keep moving.

There was one day when I got into the wrong vehicle [than the one Salem had arranged] and I ended up being drugged. I woke up in a hotel room. The phone had been removed. I didn't even know what city I was in. I was naked for the most part. There were three guys in the room. And by the time they were done gang banging me and threatening me with their firearms, the johns were knocking on the door. After about a week and a half, they had capitalized off of me as much as they possibly could.

Some traffickers try to keep the girls moving because the regular johns in that area want the new flavor of the week. The new girl in town will make a decent amount, more than regular girls. So, they tried to take me from Akron, Ohio, down to Cincinnati.

I feel like my ability to adapt helped me survive that extra little bit in certain situations, [such] as with the manipulations that had been used against me. I was able to also manipulate. I was able to talk these guys into [this]: "Okay, I'm going to come with you." I was doing everything I was told to do because I was terrified. I had gotten in their good graces and I said, "Look, I've been totally cooperative with you guys. I don't mind going to Cincinnati with you. You know, you guys have taken real good care of me. I would be able to make much more money if I can grab these outfits from the house. If I look a little cuter, we can make more money."

And they agreed. They knew they had threatened me enough. There were three of them and pistols in the car. I wasn't really much of a risk of running off. We were on the way from Akron to Cincinnati and we stopped in Columbus. I had already planned this out. We pulled up two doors away from the boyfriend's and I got out of the car and I took off running. I didn't care if they shot me in the back because I needed that boyfriend so badly. I needed to be back with him. I did not care.

Salem happened to be walking out of the apartment door and I ran up to him crying. "They drugged me, I woke up in another city, they were selling me. This is what happened." And he slapped the taste out of my mouth and dragged me in the house by my hair. He would not call the police for me. In that moment, I felt I had to do something, that these guys were up to no good. I had to call the police myself, which I did. They called an ambulance.

I want to pause for a second and tell you that these guys went on to Cincinnati and they kidnapped a fourteen year-old little girl, brought her to Columbus, and trafficked her. The main guy got four years for compelling the prostitution of a minor. This man is in his late fifties, early sixties, and is HIV positive. And he raped her. He did not get charged with rape. I have a five-year restraining order against him because he tried to come after me after he got out of prison.

Anyway, I went to the police. I went to the hospital. They did a rape kit on me and I found out I was pregnant.

I couldn't get clean (off drugs) for the life of me and I still had to work for the boyfriend. He was still using drugs in front of me when I was trying to cut back. The resources weren't available for me to get help. I had nowhere to go. I didn't know what to do. I was stuck in this. I fell deeper into my addiction, deeper into my hopelessness.

The bigger my belly got, the less money I could bring in. So, one day, he literally walked me down the street and sold me to a couple of low-level street dealers. Now, I had to work for them. He told me, "I don't know what else to do right now, because I love you and we are struggling so much. And I know that this is going to suck, but I'm still going to see you. You are right down the street and I'm still going to see you. And these guys are going to be able to take care of you and the baby."

And I was so ridiculously brainwashed that I thought it made sense for him to do that. By this point, Salem had started putting his hands on me: the physical abuse had started on top of the mental abuse.

The street dealers would dangle a little bit of drugs in front of me to keep me compliant, to keep me dependent, and to keep me moving. But I had to bring in a certain amount of money to earn extra privileges.

It was January of 2011. One night I had not made enough money to come in and rest. I had been outside for five to seven days, extremely pregnant. I was not feeling well. I was at a bus stop and it was late and this guy walked by and he was like, "Would you like to come in and get warm?" Yeah, of course. So, I walked with him and we went to his house and as soon as I sat on that couch, I fell asleep. I was exhausted. I woke up completely naked. I don't know what this guy was trying to do to me. But I know that when I tried to leave, my water broke. At some point, while I was delivering the baby myself on his floor, pulling her out of myself, he called an ambulance.

I remember putting her up on my chest. And I remember the ambulance finally coming and they took her and wrapped her in an aluminum foil type blanket. I was in and out of shock. Not only the exhaustion, but also the drug use, and giving birth myself. They had to wake me up with smelling salts in the ambulance a couple times. At the hospital, I had to be put in a medically induced coma because my blood pressure was so high. But most importantly, unfortunately, my child, of course, had to go into intensive care. She was a little over four pounds. She was highly addicted to drugs. Her Apgar score was zero. The doctor said that thank God I had the instinct to put her on my chest. It probably kept her alive. So, I'm very grateful that, yes, that baby did survive, but when I woke up from this medically induced coma, I knew, I knew there was no way I was going to be able to keep this baby.

I couldn't even keep myself, let alone keep a child. I knew that if I established a bond with this infant that I would pretty much be digging my own grave. Because I wasn't going to be able to keep her—which would have opened my wound even more. I did go down and see her for a few minutes. It was all I could stomach. It was just tearing my heart out. And I went upstairs and I left against medical advice. I did the only thing I knew how to do at that point in my life, and that was go on a strike and get high. It was the only thing that was going to numb the pain, and I felt like I was dying inside.

Because I had given birth and the guys knew it, they just kind of let me go, they knew I wasn't going to make that much money anyway.

So, where did I end up? Right back with the boyfriend. But things were a little different this time. I now realized that my prince charming was my captor. And I realized all the betrayal—the sick plays—and I was angry. So, even though I was still stuck, when he hit me, I fought back. It got to be pretty ugly, with the drug abuse and the violence. And so, he taught me the biggest lesson he ever taught me. He walked me down and sold me again, to the most violent gang in Columbus, and this was a permanent deal.

It was terrifying. It was kind of the same as with the low-level street thugs and street dealers but more intense, more violent. They had better quality crack and heroin, so they didn't have to give you as much, but you had to make more money. You had to make a very good amount of money to be allowed to use the bathroom or take a shower. And if we got caught going to the bathroom in the basement drain, we would be put out and it would not be pretty.

It was April 16th, 2013. I hadn't made enough money. I was starting to get dope sick. I was exhausted. And here came this guy. I knew the rules: You don't go turn a trick with somebody on foot.

The guys in cars have the most money. The guys on foot have less money or they are up to no good. But, you see, this guy had a pocket full of money. He showed it to me. He was good-looking; he was charismatic; he was talkative. And so, I went against the rules. I was getting sick. I thought, I'm finally going to be able to get well and get some sleep.

We went to this abandoned house and we walked in and I heard the door shut and I turned around. It wasn't the same guy: it was, but it wasn't. I saw the face of the devil, and the gleam of a butcher's knife. And, you know, my immediate thought was, "Oh, great. Let's get this over with."

I had been raped so much in that work that that was my response. I had had loaded pistols on the back of my head while I was forced to perform sex acts. I had been kicked out of moving vehicles. I had been beaten and left for dead in ditches. A huge amount of rape took place. Not just the daily buyers of rape, but the actual rapists too. So, I just thought: let's get this over with and be done with it.

He was incredibly perverted, incredibly disgusting and sick. The vile things he wanted me to do and to do to me were just stomach churning. I will spare some details, but I was vomiting on him. He was gagging me so much with his penis and, if I tried to pull away, he would punch me in the face or the head.

Anyways, it just wasn't cutting it for him. So, he took me upstairs and started raping me. That, again, was not doing it for him. He started grabbing random objects and sodomizing me with them while he was raping me. Any time I whimpered, any time I moved, I took another very hard punch to the face or upper body. I remember hearing people walking and talking and laughing outside and I couldn't do anything.

He proceeded to rape me with a butcher's knife and got me bleeding, just enough . . . . That finally did it for him. I'm grateful that when it happened, I disconnected from my body. I remember that I woke up and he was standing over me with his hand out, trying to pull my bleeding, beaten body up off the floor. We went downstairs. I put on my shorts and my bra. He left the building and I waited just a brief moment so there would be enough room between us, and I went out too.

I could still see this guy walking down the street. There were three guys getting out of their car walking up to their house as I came outside. I was beaten to the point where you couldn't tell what ethnicity I was. I was bleeding from my vagina, screaming for help. But because I was known as one of the local whores, they figured I was just mad because I didn't get my money. There'd been times when I was raped, and I asked cops for help and they would just laugh. Oh, what are you so pissed off for? He didn't pay you? So, this was kind of a repeat of that. The three men laughed at me and said we'll call the cops for you and walked off and shut the door and locked it.

The lock is what I hear echo in my mind. It was like I was being locked out of society. I was locked out of being worthy of help. I was locked out of being seen as a normal human being. As a human being, period.

I decided to run to my traffickers. I knocked on the door. The guys were out for the night, so their girlfriends were running the spot. They asked where the hell I had been. I tried explaining what happened through tears and dope sickness. I was so distraught. I had just been brutally raped for two and a half hours, I was beaten, and bleeding. I asked for the only thing I knew to ask for, ten dollars' worth of dope on credit, so that I could numb myself. Because this was all I knew. And one of them handed me three paper towels and said, "Go to the basement, clean yourself up and go out and get some money and then you can have what you want." I'd brought them hundreds of thousands of dollars and I needed ten dollars' worth of dope to curb my pain, and that's what I got.

I went downstairs. I grabbed one of the five pounds buckets that people used upside down to get high on and I went to the back corner of the basement, no light or anything. I got a rope and tied it around my neck twice. I just couldn't do it anymore. I tied the other end to the bucket and hung it from a beam, and I kicked the bucket away.

It was actually quite amazing to feel that dark, tickling warmth overcome my body, and just to feel the abuse, the rapes, the addictions, the misery—everything—just leaving out of the bottoms of my feet. It felt so good. It's to this day the one time in my life where I was pain free. And I just relaxed into it.

The only moment in her life when Jennifer felt good was when she was dying. She had suffered immensely and been dragged down into a bottomless desperation. When you have experiences like hers, it's easy to see yourself as the world sees you: not as a human being, but as a worthless junkie prostitute. Death seemed to her like a relief.

My life has been very different from Jennifer's, but I can still imagine what she felt at that moment because of my own experience of almost dying of an asthma attack all those years ago. When I came out of a deep coma after three days, I longed to be free of the need to breathe. I felt relieved that death was coming. But then it didn't come.

And Jennifer didn't die then either. We'll return to her story in a later chapter, because she has so much to teach us—about surviving the extremes of human cruelty, overcoming a brutal past, and helping other people. About vulnerability and courage. And, sadly, about relapses.

She also taught me quite a bit about the business model of modern slavery. However incapacitated she might have been by drugs, she was always sharp enough to pay attention to what was going on around her.

Among the many things Jennifer illuminated for me was how grooming works, beginning with traffickers' expertise in identifying people in vulnerable situations—be they men, women, or children—and gaining their trust over a period of time. In sex trafficking, it is the most common recruitment technique. Again and again, in countries all over the world, you hear stories of desperate people being taken under the wing of someone pretending to help, getting lulled into a sense of security, and then being sold for sex or forced work.

Cornelius Katona, Medical Director of the Helen Bamber Foundation, describes a classic Albanian grooming method: "You're the boyfriend for a year, you know everything about them, you know the numbers on their mobile phone, their family . . . anything to get power and control."

A survivor of sex trafficking in the United Kingdom, a woman we'll call Sarah, was groomed in a similar way in England. Her grooming began when she was an extremely vulnerable ten-year-old living in foster care, with no stable family or homelife. Her slavers were seasoned and very good at it. These apparently kindly men—members of a gang, she later learned—approached her with offers of sweets, rides in their cars, light drugs. When her foster parents disappeared for days at a time, these men would feed her. When she was sad, they brought her gifts. The gang "looked after her" very attentively, generous with their friendship and smiles. Sarah describes feeling loved and having a sense of community for the first time in her life—something she'd craved.

But when she was twelve, they told her she had to pay them back for everything they'd bought and done for her—a total of £75,000, by their calculations. They showed her photographs of her friends and family and said they'd be shot if she told anyone what was going on.

They started by having Sarah transport and sell drugs, but when she proved to be incompetent at that work because she was too scared, they forced her into sex slavery. For the next seven years, she was made to have sex with between seven and sixteen men every day.

Another thing Jennifer taught me is that for traffickers, preying on former victims is a very tempting proposition. If a woman falls into forced prostitution again, it is much less work than grooming new girls— or boys, who can be sex trafficked under these exact same conditions— into the business. So, they re-recruit former slaves whenever they can.

One reason this re-recruitment works so well is that many trafficking victims have criminal records—for prostitution, drugs, or petty theft, because their traffickers often denied them sufficient food or clothing. Jennifer had been charged for stealing two pairs of underwear; her traffickers wouldn't even pay for that. And because she had that theft on her record, it was very difficult for her to get a job after she'd escaped and started to get clean of the drugs.

When the authorities treat these victims as criminals and prostitutes, they are much more likely to fall back into slavery because they have no other options. It's only very recently that law enforcement and the judicial system have started to understand that prostitutes are not always doing it by choice, that a very large number of them are trafficked and forced into the business. Cyrus Vance Jr., the district attorney for Manhattan, told me that for the first twenty years of his career as a prosecutor, he thought they were all there of their own will.

The fact that the vast majority of victims have been addicted to hard drugs also makes it easy for traffickers to reassert control over them. Indeed, addiction is an almost universal recruitment technique. As we learned from Jennifer, her heroin and crack addictions were key to her enslavement—and very intentional on the part of her trafficker. A survivor getting out of a rehabilitation center, wondering where she is going to live and how to earn some money, is the perfect prey. A trafficker might wait hours outside of a detox center or a jail when he learns a former victim is getting released. Ready to "help."

The victims who are lucky enough to escape the hell of slavery then face isolation, poverty, no job prospects, and sometimes homelessness, as the state only takes care of them for a short while, if at all. In the United States, for instance, the government will provide a maximum of forty-five days of shelter and treatment, in the best of cases. On top of that, most victims have untreated post-traumatic stress disorder (PTSD), because to date very few treatment or rehabilitation programs understand the psychology of enslavement.

All of these circumstances mean that victims' PTSD is frequently triggered. However hard they've been working to stay clean and sober, when something triggers them, they want to numb the emotional pain. And without adequate treatment, many survivors know only one way to do that: drugs. Relapsing often puts them back in the vicinity of their traffickers because they go back to the same streets to purchase the narcotics. In moments like these, survivors are incredibly vulnerable, and traffickers will take the opportunity to re-traffic them.

From the trafficker's perspective, such a person is easier to manipulate than a new "recruit." It might only take a day or two, or the promise of food, a roof, a shower, or drugs, to convince them to go back on the street. Plus, a former victim already knows the routine, and, in most cases, they don't feel they are worth anything. They are easy money, and traffickers, often themselves drug addicts, will always choose the lazy and easy way to get control of a person.

Jennifer's colleagues at Survivor's Ink explain that this is one of the biggest challenges they face: When a survivor leaves a detoxification facility in Ohio, they should be sent to a care facility in California or somewhere else thousands of miles away, so none of their traffickers can reach them. The NGO wants to create a network of survivor-leaders across the United States for this purpose. We will speak of this again in the solutions chapter.

Sex trafficking is a rapidly growing business, in large part because it is so easy to put ads online and to sell people on websites that, by definition, have no borders.

Evidence from police forces across the globe suggests that criminals are now either moving from drugs into sex trafficking, or expanding their drug trade to include sex, because there is so little risk they'll get caught. Moreover, it's extremely lucrative. You can sell a girl many times a day, with consistent profits. That's why the business is probably much bigger than the ILO figure of $150 billion.

For instance, French law enforcement agencies estimate that in France alone the online sex business is worth $3 billion a year, and while there is little information on what percentage of that is slavery, it is believed to be significant. In a country of 66 million people, only a minority of them use these kinds of services. But even if we use only a fraction of this number as an average for most countries around the world, it is clear that the business of global trafficking certainly far exceeds $150 billion in profit a year.

Whatever the exact global profit, it's painfully clear that it's large, and the reason for that is easy to guess: As with any business, in human trafficking, income generation is key. Greed is the driver spurring on traffickers to make even bigger profits from those they enslave. Corruption is the grease without which this business would not exist—from the corrupt police officer, to the ignorant flight attendant; from the CEO who doesn't want to see the forced labor in his supply chain, to the justice system that doesn't enforce the laws forbidding slavery in every country in the world. Greed, corruption, and ignorance are the engines of modern slavery.

The lack of accurate data helps the traffickers and, of course, thwarts the agencies and individuals trying to fight slavery. It highlights three things:

First, we have probably only uncovered the tip of the iceberg when it comes to counting the number of slaves in the world today. Second, this lack of data makes it impossible to measure progress or failure in addressing the issue. And it makes it very difficult for the brave NGOs on the front lines to get funding, because it's hard for them to demonstrate their impact. Third, it shows us that slavery is a well-organized crime, and yet we fight it in a totally disorganized manner.

Mary Fischer, who was executive director of Survivor's Ink, says traffickers in Ohio make six figures a year, consistently. Their overhead is incredibly low, with a steady supply of victims who cost little to nothing in living expenses. The girls and women often sleep on basement floors—but only after they've earned enough on the street to pay the trafficker to be let back inside, where they are often not even allowed a shower.

That detail about the shower might seem insignificant, but I've heard many times from survivors, including Jennifer, that in order to debase and sully them further, traffickers systematically deny their victims the ability to get clean. All over the world, the very first thing a victim usually does when she finally arrives at a shelter is to ask for a shower.

In both sex trafficking and forced labor, false promises of well-paid work are another common recruitment method. Brokers in Myanmar will promise men good jobs cutting trees in Thailand, but when they arrive there they are put onto boats and trapped at sea for months, catching the fish that we eat in the West. It is the first time many of them see waves, as they often come from mountainous inland terrain, and they are terrified. But that is just the start of their ordeal. They soon discover that they have to work sixteen hours a day for months on end for no pay.

In Nepal, the poorest country in Asia since the earthquake of 2015, parents sometimes choose to send their children off to situations where they are promised an education as well as a paying job. None of it is true, of course, and the child can be sold to a brothel in Kathmandu, sent to India as an unpaid domestic, or sent to the Gulf region as a laborer on a construction site.

The same thing occurs in India. Alpana Rawat, a young woman who works with the Nobel Peace Prize winner Kailash Satyarthi in his ashram in Rajasthan, told me how recruitment works there: "The trafficker influences the parents and says, 'I will take your child, I will give him a good quality of life, a good education, but he will have to do just a little bit of work and I will pay you two thousand rupees per month.' The parents receive no money, or only once or twice at the start. The child has been transferred from Delhi to Bihar, and it's very far. The parents can't travel. They don't even have enough money to buy food."

Very often, it's someone you know and trust who sells you into slavery—a family friend, an uncle, or an aunt—who acts as a broker. Evelyn Chumbow, who has become a friend and who you will meet again in my heroes chapter, lived the first nine years of her life with her parents in Cameroon, Africa, until her uncle sold her to a family in the United States. He had promised her parents she would have a good education and a shiny American life, and that she would only have to "help around the house." Her uncle told Evelyn that the mother in the family would be like a mother to her.

It could not have been further from the truth. Evelyn was put to work all day, every day, and soon after she arrived, the physical abuse began. She was never sent to school. She was not allowed to leave the house, except for errands. She was enslaved, pure and simple.

Once the victims are in the hands of traffickers, there are many methods for keeping them there, and for extracting the most work out of them. In other industries, this would be called "training." Human traffickers approach it more like breaking horses: to wear their chattel down in body and in spirit. A rebellious slave is a poor business proposition, so it is important that the slaveholder be able to ensure compliance and docility in their asset.

How do they actually get the slaves to stay and to do the work? As with historical slavery, the most common and probably the most effective method is threats of violence or death to the slave or his or her loved ones. As we heard from Sarah in the United Kingdom, the gang threatened to kill her family and friends if she told anyone—and what is so powerful about this kind of threat is that it not only ensures the victim's silence, but also her cooperation. Certainly, Sarah feared for her life for the entire seven years of her enslavement, and rightly so. In Columbus, Ohio, where Jennifer was trafficked, traffickers would lock girls, women, and sometimes boys and men in basements, numbed by drugs and menaced by pit bulls. These threats happen all the time in forced labor, too, as the New York district attorney's office has found.

In order to demonstrate that the threats are serious, assert their power, and break the spirit of the enslaved person, slaveholders almost always abuse their victims physically with beatings, cigarette burns, and the like. But they are also careful about it, according to Professor Katona: "They make sure that their victims continue to be work productive, whether that's sex work or domestic work, and they subjugate and hurt them just enough, and they make sure that the wounds don't show."

Then there is rape, a prevailing form of violence and domination in modern slavery. Rape is often used repeatedly by multiple men. It's common practice that when a trafficked girl is sold to a new gang, she will be raped by all the members to demonstrate their ownership of her.

It doesn't just occur in sex trafficking. Kevin Bales has found that virtually all women in slavery are raped, including in situations of forced labor. Nor does it only happen to women: Indonesian fishermen working on foreign-chartered vessels have reported that, in addition to having their passports taken and being at sea for months on end, they were routinely sexually abused by the officers onboard. Every specialist with whom I've spoken says that people who are trafficked and physically abused for work will most likely be abused sexually as well, somewhere along the road. One expert describes sexual abuse as part of the commercial enterprise of slavery—systematized in many ways, often including giving victims birth control, as we see among the girls and women used as sex slaves by Daesh, a terrorist organization that for a few years took control of entire cities in Iraq and Syria.

Unsurprisingly, rape is an extremely effective tool for subjugating slaves. Repeated sexual assault by their slavers sinks victims deep into shame. Because there is no rational explanation for why this is happening to them, they begin to blame themselves and lose their sense of self-worth.

Later in the book we'll look more at what mental health specialists call "traumatic bonding," which happens when victims of abuse lose their sense of self-worth to such an extreme degree that they believe they deserve mistreatment, or that the abuse somehow shows that they are loved: "If he didn't love me so much, he wouldn't get so angry." When a traumatic bond has developed, the abuse can actually reinforce the connection the victim feels with the abuser.

This phenomenon is very common in domestic violence and it is the main reason why people stay in dangerous situations. In sex trafficking, it's a tried-and-true part of the business model. During Jennifer's grooming, Salem planted the seeds for her twisted, but nonetheless powerful, attachment to him, and it proved an effective method of inducing her to stay with him and work for him.

There are many other methods of increasing the victims' vulnerability and the traffickers' power. Professor Katona says, "The traffickers are very sophisticated. They recognize vulnerability a mile off. And they use the most culturally appropriate methods. In Nigeria, they will very often use witchcraft because that is something that they know to be in the culture of their victims. In Albania it's very much about the family and so they will say, 'If you don't do what I say I will do the same to your sister.'"

Traffickers also maintain power over their victims by removing their freedom of movement. When people are brought across international borders, whether legally or not, their traffickers take possession of their passports and other travel documents, and of course of their phones. From individual cases of domestic slavery, to the international sex trade, to construction companies in Gulf countries and elsewhere, this universal method is one of the most powerful tools for ensuring slaves don't try to escape.

We also heard from Jennifer how one of the gangs that trafficked her would move their slaves around to different towns or neighborhoods every week or so, because the customers will pay more for new women and girls whom they call "fresh meat." This happens on a larger, international scale, too. A survivor we will meet later in the book was trafficked from Latin America to Japan for the same reason: Japanese men seem to like white women from Latin America and Europe.

Compared to the sale of sex via the Internet, brothels and street trade seem old-fashioned and relatively small. The trade in violence against women and children has migrated and expanded online worldwide, with the help of user-friendly websites where children are sold outright. These sites also sell so-called "child pornography," though we must stop using that term because such pornography doesn't exist: these children are not making porn; they are sex-abuse victims. Later in the book we'll look at the 2018 U.S. law that aimed at preventing online sex trafficking and that finally put the notorious site Backpage.com out of business and its boss, into jail.

The websites that sell human beings online are many—all over the world—and with the emergence of social media, more and more children and teenagers risk falling into the hands of traffickers. In October 2017, U.S. authorities rescued eighty-four children, one just three months old, and arrested 120 people in a nationwide sweep of child sex slavery that exposed the growing use of technology by traffickers. Many of those arrested were advertising and selling the children online.

In *I Am Jane Doe*, the extraordinary documentary by Mary Mazzio, we see how Jane's mother discovered her missing teenage daughter on Backpage.com. She almost had a heart attack: Jane was selling herself for sex services. Eventually, she understood that her daughter had been trafficked and this was why she had vanished a year earlier.

We can't discuss sex trafficking or forced labor without looking at refugees, who comprise a steady supply for traffickers. The world is currently experiencing the largest human migration since World War II, providing endless opportunities to take control of vulnerable children, women, and men. More than 68 million people are displaced today—25 million because of wars and conflicts—and traffickers are capitalizing on that fact. Whether you are a Syrian mother or a Rohingya father, it is the safety of your family that matters most to you. You would do anything, even accept a suspicious job offer, to earn a living so you could get your children to safety and keep them housed and fed.

And situations don't have to be as extreme as what is happening in Syria or Myanmar to create the right conditions for slavery. People of all different means and circumstances can end up in desperate situations because of war, natural disasters, scarcity of water, poverty, and so on. Sixty million people have been on the move since about 2010. And when it happens and you have to migrate—be it from Africa to Europe, from Central America to the United States, or within Asia— the dangers you meet are all too similar. Undocumented women making their way to the country they dream of are easy prey for smugglers of all kinds. Traffickers prey upon them. It is vulnerability that turns people into slaves.

3

From Nepal to Qatar

Debt Bondage

It was the desperate need for a job that led Deependra Giri into slavery. He was a well-educated Nepalese with teaching experience, he spoke five languages, including good English, and knew how to use computers: all qualities that should have kept him from falling prey to slavery. And yet, at a particularly vulnerable moment in his life, he was trafficked from his home in a remote village in Nepal to an industrial site in Qatar where he was trapped for more than two years.

Deependra and I have kept in close touch ever since he spoke at the Trust Women Conference in 2013, when he shared his experience as a slave in Qatar. I mentioned him earlier as the man whose debt was paid off by a woman who heard him speak there, a life-changing gift. Deependra and I were introduced by Andrew Gardner, an American professor who documented labor practices and conditions in the Emirates.

During his off-hours in Qatar, Deependra secretly worked with Gardner, taking photographs and gathering testimonies of other laborers in his camp. Gardner was a visiting professor at Qatar University. If Deependra had been caught documenting the site, his life would have been in danger. Likewise, Gardner would have at least jeopardized his teaching position if he'd been caught poking around in the labor camps. The companies in the Gulf that perpetrate slavery are very careful to keep outsiders away, which keeps their crimes in the shadows.

Deependra was trapped in what is called "debt bondage" or "bonded labor," which is the most common form of slavery today. The ILO estimates that 50 percent of people enslaved by individuals are ensnared in some type of debt bondage. It can assume many shapes, but in the basic model a victim takes a loan from someone, usually at a madly inflated interest rate, and when they cannot pay it back, they have to work for practically no pay until the debt is repaid: essentially, they are collateral against the loan.

When he spoke at the 2013 conference, it had only been a couple of years since Deependra had regained his freedom, and he was still deeply shaken by his experience. A very polite man, he was shy but gave a clear description of how he had been trapped. He even showed us a few photos he had taken of the dreadful building where the slaves were kept, a few kilometers from Doha, Qatar's capital.

Sometimes, they had to sleep on the tin roof because the heat was so suffocating. They would wake up caked in white dust from the cement factory next door.

Over the next few years, as Deependra recovered and gained confidence, I came to understand that he is actually a very outgoing and chatty man. He came back to the conference in 2014 to explain how he was now building his own NGO in Nepal. And then, in 2017, he went back to Qatar to determine if there had been any progress since his work with Andrew Gardner. He saw some improvements, but slavery was still rampant.

When I next saw him, in Washington, DC, for my conference in April 2017, he was completely transformed. He had become self-confident and seemed almost a different person than the one I'd first met four years earlier. He felt good about himself, wore an elegant tweed jacket, a lovely tie, and big glasses that made him look like an academic. Deependra has delicate manners and is full of warmth and energy. These qualities had always been in his nature, but they had been squashed in the years during and after he was trafficked. His innate high spirits, together with his intelligence, diligence, and computer skills, were probably what led the recruitment agency in Nepal to choose him from among hundreds of job seekers.

What the recruiters didn't see, however, were his resilience and his compassion. If they'd known that he would help his fellow forced workers, they probably wouldn't have "hired" him. And they definitely wouldn't have selected someone who was going to use his one day off each week to document the widespread labor abuses in Qatar.

In 2017, the two of us sat down like old friends so I could take down his entire story as he now recollects it.

Here is the first part of what he told me, in his own words:

Before my marriage I was doing three jobs—working as a teacher at a primary school, doing home tutoring, and teaching computer classes. Back then, I was able to take care of myself. But after I got married in 2005, my financial problems started to become bigger. I started looking for better opportunities. I tried a lot but couldn't find anything in Nepal.

In 2008, I became a father. I started applying for jobs in Gulf countries—I used to go through the newspapers every day; there were a lot of advertisements. One day I saw one for a clerk job in Qatar. Ninety percent of the recruiting agencies' advertisements are for construction jobs and only 10 percent are indoor jobs. I decided to apply for it.

The advertisement clearly stated that the visa and plane ticket would be provided by the company; I wouldn't have to pay anything for those. The processing fee was only 20,000 rupees (US $200). I didn't know the tricks of these recruiting agencies. I went to Kathmandu and gave them copies of my passport and my CV. They said they'd call to tell me when the interview would take place.

I got a call ten days later that I had a pre-interview in Kathmandu in two days. That is a very hard thing to accomplish for people living outside the capital. I live 300 kilometers away. It took me ten hours to get there, and it was very expensive.

I went and had the pre-interview with one of the recruiting agency staff. There were more than 500 people there, for one vacancy only. I went back home and after two days they gave me a call and said, "Deependra, you've been selected and you have to be here for the final interview."

The final interview was with a Syrian guy from the company in Qatar. After some conversation he told me, "Deependra, congratulations, I have selected you." He was treating me like a friend, so I said, "Can I ask you a question? There were 500 people and many of the ones I spoke with were more intelligent and more educated and better at English than me." He said, "I was going through the CVs and I don't know why but I liked your CV and so I selected you." I thanked him. He said my salary would be QAR 1200 (US $330), I would get food and accommodation, and they would send me all the details and the visa.

I was happy, but in another way I was not feeling good because I did not want to leave my daughter and my wife Sunita. Aayushi was just one month old, and it was my responsibility to look after both of them. I was confused about what to do.

Should I stay and look after them? But to look after them properly, I needed money. I talked to my parents and my in-laws and they said, "Don't worry, Deependra, we will take care of them. You just go and do your job."

I contacted my recruiting agency and they said I should talk to the sub-agent in my area. I was confused, because until then I'd been in touch with the recruitment agency directly. Later, I came to know that recruitment agencies in Kathmandu have sub-agents all over Nepal. The sub-agent said I had to give him around US $1200 for various fees and for my plane ticket, though the advert had said the company would pay for it.

I also learned much later that at some of the giant companies in Qatar, the human resources managers, who usually work closely with the company owners, negotiate with recruiting agencies in Nepal.

"I have 100 visas for laborers, how much will you pay me per head?" They probably negotiate US $500 per visa. In the beginning, that is paid by the recruiter, but later they charge the worker for it.

And I didn't have a piece of land or anything I could sell. I was twenty-five or twenty-six years old and I was still living in my grandparents' house. It's very hard to get a loan from the bank if you don't own anything.

So, I took an individual loan from one of my neighbors who ran a money-lending business. He knew everything about me, so it was a matter of trust, and I assured him that I would pay the interest. We signed a paper in front of a lawyer and the interest rate was very low, very nominal. But, later that day, the neighbor asked me to come back to his home and sign another paper that was not official, and that said I had to pay 60 percent interest.

I had to sign it or else they were not going to give me the money. I got the money and prepared for my journey and did some shopping for clothes, a toothbrush, soap, and shampoo.

I was ready to go. I didn't have a mobile phone at that time. Everyone was worried about how they would know I got to Qatar safely. And I said, "I will try to find someone at the airport and will give you a call."

I flew to Qatar and when I got off the flight at 11:00 at night, it was so hot that, for a second, I was confused. Nepal is very hot, but it was even hotter here. I thought, how am I going to stay here for two years? But I said to myself, no worries, I paid a lot of money and did so many things to get here, now I have to stay.

After I got through Immigration, a guy came up and said, "Deependra?" and I said, "Yes," and he said, "Give me your passport." He takes my passport. I wonder what is going to happen to me; I don't know this guy. He asks me to sit in a white Mitsubishi van. Sometimes I still dream about that van and it's like I have seen it in a scary movie. He didn't talk to me much. He just drove and drove and drove. And then I could see the desert with no trees, no houses. Once, he stopped at a gas station and got me some food. He said I could eat in the car, but I told him I could not do that, and asked if we could sit in the restaurant. He smiled and said okay.

Finally, we reached the labor camp in the industrial area, where females are not allowed to go. He took me to a building and said this was my accommodation, but it looked more like a warehouse. We went inside and I could see rats bigger than cats moving here and there. There were tires everywhere. And, in the middle, there were some beds. Many people were sleeping there. He said, "This is your bed, Deependra, and you can take rest." I said, "Can I take a shower?" And he smiled and said, "Oh, there is no electricity, so the bathroom is dark and it's better if you shower in the morning." There was also no drinking water.

I tried to sleep, but I could not. I was homesick and on top of that there was this scary accommodation. I remembered that I had to call my family. But I thought, what is the use of calling them if I'm just going to cry continuously. I decided I would call them tomorrow and say that I'd been tired and had forgot.

In the morning, when I woke up, I introduced myself to the guy in the next bed and we discovered we were both from Rupandehi Bhairahawa. I was so happy, at least someone was from the same place as me.

First thing I asked him: "If you have a mobile, can I borrow it to call my family? They must be worried from last night." And he said sure. I forgot about the scary accommodation, because I had a friend now. I called my wife and said, "Everything is very fine," and she asked me, "How is your accommodation?" I said, "Oh, you can't believe how good it is."

What was I going to say? She cannot help me. My parents, neither. And I didn't want to make them panic. So, I told them, "I had fantastic food last night" and blah, blah, blah. And she was happy.

My manager was a Palestinian guy. The day after I arrived he took me to a warehouse full of spare parts of big trucks and cranes and heavy machinery. He told me I'd work in here. I told him that I was selected to work as a clerk and he said, "Yes, but we already have a clerk, so you have to work here." And I said okay, it's fine, because what can I do? I wasn't mentally or physically prepared for that kind of labor. But I had travelled a long way, my family was far away, I didn't know anyone to ask for help. So, under any conditions I was going to work there, because I had signed a contract that said I could not leave the country until I completed two years of work.

Due to the Kafala system in Qatar you cannot leave a job if you don't like it. You have to complete the contract. So, even if I got my passport back, I would still have needed to get an exit permit from my sponsor or I wouldn't have been allowed to leave the country. I didn't know where my passport was, and I was very scared about that.

On my second day, the office manager told me to clean his car and his friend's car. I took cleaning supplies and got started. It was hard because of the heat, and it was lunch time and I'd had no breakfast, but I couldn't tell him anything because I was new. After I cleaned the car he said, "You don't know how to clean a car." I said, "Sir, I don't own a car in my home country, so I don't know how to clean a car."

I had been promised US $330, but I found out I would be getting only $275, with no breakfast, and no meals at all on the day off, which was Friday. I said to my manager, "Sir, in my agreement it says I get food and accommodation, but we don't get food on Friday." He said, "You're not working for us on Friday."

For a month or two, I did odd jobs, moving furniture and spare parts. After a while, another manager came and said, "Deependra, what are you doing? We hired you as a clerk." So, the next day, I went to the office and he asked me if I knew how to write letters, make Excel sheets, and make individual files. I said yes.

My first task was to go through a list of workers and make a file for each one. There were more than 600 people. The documents were not managed well. Someone's passport copy would be in one file, and who knows where their medical report was. It took around one month to make the 600 files.

I managed to do it in such a way that the manager was very happy. And when Jim, the general manager, came, he too was so happy and told me, "Deependra, I am impressed by your work and, so, I am going to increase your salary to 1500 riyals (US $412). You go to your desk and you just send the manager in."

What they talked about, I don't know. When my manager came out, I told him, "Sir, Jim told me to write a letter saying that my salary has been increased, and he will sign it." He said, "No, I talked to him. For the time being it's okay as you are. We will talk later."

So, at the beginning it was hard. I was shouted at every day, and I feared being beaten like they did to other workers. I didn't receive my first month's salary. I had to pay back the debt. I said to my manager, "Sir, I need money to send back home and to pay back what I have borrowed from people, and I have to pay interest and all these things." He said, "Ok, we will pay you your salary." But instead he gave me about fifty riyals for pocket money. The second month came, and it was the same story: no salary. Third month: no salary. By then I was thinking of suicide.

What could I do? We had a baby, and they would not pay me. The moneylender was continuously asking my wife when I would send the money. I didn't have pocket money. I didn't have money to call my parents. I didn't have money to give to my wife for her personal expenses. And I could not ask my parents to give her money because things are very different in my country. In our society, people would laugh at you. I thought suicide would be the best solution.

Then, one of my friends gave me his salary and said I could pay him back when I got mine. I was very thankful to him. Eventually I started getting paid, but only one month's salary every three months.

Whenever one of us received our salary, we sent money home in rotation. My three friends would give me their salaries one month and I would send it home. The next pay, I would do the same with them. The first thing we did was pay three months of my interest, and I sent 3,000 rupees (US $29) to my wife. But this is not enough when there is a small baby.

But slowly I started feeling more comfortable in that place. After four or five months, my manager said, "Now, I am going to give you the responsibility of the salary sheets and the overtime money of the other workers." I had to calculate their overtime money. I started doing it and, suddenly, the overtime money was increased because the manager had told the clerk before me not to count all the overtime money. But I did not know that. And why should I cheat the other employees? So, I just calculated whatever they were owed.

My manager said, "Deependra, this is crazy. How can a driver make 5,000 riyals?" I said, "Oh, it's per the overtime sheet you gave me. I can check and you can calculate." He said, "You have to deduct that and make it 2200. I don't know how you are going to do it, but you are going to do it." I did what he said. I submitted it to him. It was my duty to get the money from the bank and pay everyone.

A few drivers went to the manager and said, "Sir, we are owed more than that." He said, "I don't know, Deependra is dealing with this, talk to him. Whatever he calculates, I sign. It's up to him, not me." That was why he asked me to do it, so I would be responsible for it.

That evening, I went to my room and I saw a lot of people waiting for me. I was very friendly with them, but that day they were looking at me as if I was their biggest enemy. They said, "Why do you make this salary sheet?"

I said to the men, "I am only putting it on the computer and this data is given to me by the manager. If you don't trust me, let's go talk face-to-face with him. And you will know if I am telling the truth or he is telling the truth." The next day they went to the office and said, "We talked to Deependra and this is not Deependra's fault. This is your fault. So, either you give us the full payment, or we will go on a strike." I gave them that idea the evening before.

The manager kept it pending for a long time. He said, "Take this amount and later we will pay you the remaining amount that we owe." So, they said, "Okay, we can wait," and went back to work and things returned to normal.

In the meantime, they changed our accommodation. They learned that an inspection was going to happen in the industrial area and if the inspectors found us staying in that warehouse, then the company would have to pay a huge amount of money and they might be put in jail. They moved us to a building at the end of the industrial area. The ground floor had no electricity, and the first and second floors were under construction. Even in my country you cannot live somewhere that is under construction.

So, the next day we went to the office. I said to my manager, "It is under construction. There is nothing. We were not able to take showers because there is no water. If it stays this way, we are going to be ill." And he said, "Look, we are trying to arrange everything for you." But they didn't.

One day, I met Andrew Gardner in the industrial area. A friend of mine introduced us. Andrew was a visiting professor to Qatar

University and he used to come to the industrial area to see how things were, to take photographs, to talk to people. He didn't have an assistant.

The biggest problem for him was that he was the guy with the whitest skin, and you do not see any white people in the industrial area. It was very hard for him to go to the camps and get anything done. And so, he asked me if I'd like to work for him on my day off. He said he would pay me.

We planned to meet the next Friday. He took me for breakfast. It was the first time in months I really had a good breakfast. He told me that my job would be to find people with problems and to interview them, to record them, to transcribe and send it to him. He also wanted me to take photographs for him, if possible. I said I could take photographs.

And, so, we started our project together. I was very excited. Nobody knew about it. I started finding people, talking to them, interviewing them, making reports.

The first payment I received from Andrew, I used to buy my laptop, which I still have. I bought it in 2008. It is no longer in good condition, but I still manage to work with it. I love that laptop.

The payment from Andrew was more than what I got from the office! It encouraged me to work harder and give more time for his project. We would take people in his car because it was the safest place to interview anyone.

I speak Nepali, Hindi, Bhojpuri, Awadhi. I translated into English for Andrew. He would give the people we interviewed a recharge card and a small sack of rice, and 30 riyals an hour for their time. They were happy.

And I was slowly telling Andrew about the problems we were facing in the office. He said, "If you need anything, just let me know."

The drivers were still waiting for the remaining money and one day they went on strike. The manager suspended them. Their

salary was stopped. Their food was stopped. They were in real
trouble. It was four or five Nepalese, two or three Indians, and a
few Bangladeshis. They came to my room and said, "What can we
do now?" I told them, "Let me think. Don't worry about the food,
you guys can have some of ours. But make sure that the manager
doesn't know."

I had money now, from working with Andrew. Every week I
sent money home to my wife and she said, "Oh my God, Deependra, some time ago you did not have money and now you are
sending me every week." She sent me photos of our daughter in
the mail. I still didn't have a cell phone. A few Bangladeshis managed to operate illegal Internet calls. It was one riyal to call home
for six or seven minutes. I used this to talk with my family and
every time they said, "We are fine. We have everything. Everything is good here."

At my next meeting with Andrew, I spoke about our problem:
"The drivers went on strike and the company suspended them.
We don't know what to do." and he said, "Let me talk to a few
people and I will get back to you. But until then just tell them to
keep quiet. It's not like Nepal here; tell them not to go and say
any bad words to the manager or beat anyone. If you do these
things here, you will be in real trouble and no one will be able
to help you."

Poverty is one of the main conditions that puts people at higher risk
of being trafficked. Benjamin Skinner, a journalist who now runs an
anti-trafficking NGO called Transparentem, put it to me this way: "Not
everybody who is poor is a slave. But extreme economic vulnerability
makes it more likely that you are going to be in a situation where your
social fabric is ruptured. And when you are in a new situation, away
from those who really love you, you are more prone to being exploited.
You are more prone to becoming a slave." As Deependra's experience

shows, anyone, anywhere, can be forced into slavery if they fall into financial difficulty.

Deependra's debt bondage also demonstrates how different aspects of the trafficking business model can overlap and interact. I'm constantly astonished by slavery's endless permutations and the slippery and inventive machinations of slavers in almost every industry and country.

Deependra was subject to an intricate, diffuse sort of debt bondage, involving multiple contracts he signed with the recruitment agency, the moneylender, and the company in Qatar. Forced-labor traffickers like to use the modern labor practice of contracts to conceal their traffic, both from the victim—who doesn't understand what is actually happening until much too late—and from the authorities, should they take notice.

Each paper Deependra signed only served to increase his debt and curtail his freedom, directly or indirectly. Although he was not indebted to the company, but rather to the lender in Nepal, the company certainly knew that workers coming from impoverished countries had to take big loans at sky-high interest rates in order to pay for their airfare—plus whatever else they had to pay for a home.

To be sure, its workers' debt was part of the company's business model: Promise a decent wage, then severely underpay workers so that they can never repay their debt and therefore have to keep working. The debt, together with the fact that the company could decide if and when to give workers exit permits to leave Qatar or simply take their holiday, was an extremely effective way to keep people trapped in the company's dubious employ. They literally could not leave.

As Deependra mentioned, the exit permits are part of the Kafala, or sponsorship, system firmly in place throughout the Gulf countries. The Kafala system requires local companies to sponsor their foreign workers in order to validate their work visas and residency. I'll discuss this strategy more later in the book, but basically it puts foreign workers completely at the mercy of companies and leaves plenty of room for exploitation.

Under the Kafala system, however abusive the situation—employers can take workers' passports, give them meals of dog food, force them to work fifteen-hour days in extreme heat, and house them in horrendous living conditions—the worker has no legal recourse. If the worker escapes a bad situation, he cannot leave the country until the company grants him an exit permit, nor is he allowed to get another job within the country. It is entirely up to the company to decide when and whether to give its workers exit permits. The system not only paves the way for human trafficking, but also provides cover for it.

In addition to worker debt and the Kafala system, the company that enslaved Deependra used another very effective business strategy: bureaucratic chaos. All the broken promises and conflicting information from various dodgy managers always benefited the company and exploited the laborers. Some were obviously part of a company strategy of hiding malfeasance under the cover of chaos, like the lower-than-stated salary and the severely inadequate housing and food. But even if other, less-egregious instances—such as the confusion over Deependra's exact role—were genuinely the result of chaotic management rather than deliberate exploitation, the managers were in complete control of the workers and so always turned any confusion to their own advantage. Surely it was not in Deependra's job description to clean people's cars under the punishing Gulf sun.

Corruption also played a big role in Deependra's enslavement. As he described learning after the fact, the human resources staff at some Gulf companies have secret relationships with recruiters in South Asia. That means that a large portion of the money Deependra had to pay the sub-agent in Nepal may well have gone into the pocket of someone at the company that hired him, rather than to cover his supposed expenses—corruption, pure and simple. And even in cases where the hiring company is not directly colluding with recruitment agencies in corrupt and illegal practices, the companies are undoubtedly aware of the generally dishonest, often unlawful, methods of Nepalese agencies that profit by charging workers all sorts of extra processing and placement fees. It only serves to benefit the companies: the greater a worker's debt, the longer he can be exploited.

The fabrication and exploitation of debt has been adopted in many iterations of slavery, all over the world. In traditional debt bondage, the slave is indebted directly to the slaveholder. It's a widely established practice in some countries, and there are guiding rules—which, of course, always benefit the master. Sometimes, the debt can never be repaid because it is increased every time the enslaved person needs a doctor or medicine or anything else, and, in these cases, it can be inherited by the slave's children, and sometimes even by their grandchildren. In India, Pakistan, Nepal, and Sri Lanka, millions of people are trapped in this hereditary debt bondage, with generation after generation born into it.

The most diabolical part of it is that every aspect of repayment is determined entirely by the slaveholder: They decide the interest rate. They decide how much work it will take to pay off the loan and how much is added to the debt for things like food, housing, medical treatment, and travel to worksites. They can decide at any moment to increase the interest rate; I have heard of rates as high as 300 percent in India. Of course, violence or the threat of it is often used in conjunction with debt to coerce the slaves into staying.

Some Nepalese survivors rescued from slavery working in brick kilns told a group of us that they had no idea they were enslaved. They thought it was normal that their master beat them and fed them like dogs. They never thought life could be different.

South Asia is not the only place where people are still born into slavery. In Africa, Mauritania's ongoing hereditary bondage system is carried out openly and remains deeply embedded in society. Biram Dah Abeid, an active abolitionist whose mother remained a slave and whose father had been emancipated, spoke about it at our 2016 conference. Roughly 17 percent of Mauritania's population is enslaved today and receives no education. The government officially outlawed slavery in 1981—the last country in the world to do so—but it continues unfettered. Biram was arbitrarily jailed again in 2018 to bar him from playing a role in the elections in Mauritania.

In Haiti, the site of the modern world's first and only successful slave revolt (in 1791, just two years after the French Revolution), institutionalized slavery still exists to this day. Children known as *restaveks* (translated literally as "stay-withs") are sent by their parents to live with more affluent families. Or they are sold by brokers to anyone who wants to buy them for a handful of dollars. Ben Skinner witnessed this himself: While conducting research in Haiti, he was offered a ten-year-old girl for $50. The alleged arrangement is that the children do domestic work in exchange for better living conditions and opportunities like food, housing, and education. In reality, most *restaveks* are slaves, fed just enough to keep them working, beaten frequently, raped, and deprived of any freedom of movement, contact with parents, or education.

Finally, we cannot forget the plight of thousands of political prisoners in the laogai (labor camp) system in China. It's highly unusual for any government today to participate in institutionalized slavery, but that is the case in mainland China.

Chen Guangcheng, the blind lawyer and human rights activist famous for his daring escape from house arrest in China, spent four years in one of these prisons. He was imprisoned for organizing a class-action suit against local authorities and their brutal enforcement of the one-child policy—which included forced sterilization, forced abortions at all stages of pregnancy, and even killing newborn babies.

At the 2017 Trust Conference (previously called the Trust Women Conference), Chen recounted that prisoners were commonly forced to work twelve to sixteen hours a day, sometimes with meager compensation, sometimes with none at all. They were expected to fill impossible quotas, making products such as Christmas lights, disposable plastic gloves, and sweets. When they inevitably failed to meet their quotas, they were tortured. "The cries of people being beaten became a common background noise in jail," said Chen.

Prison officials make good money off of this system, resulting in a market for inmates, regularly sold between facilities for a few hundred to a few thousand yen. Some of Chen's fellow inmates were traded in this way. The head of the prison where he had been held said it's like this everywhere in China. But, of course, the government keeps the laogai system under wraps, so there is almost no information publicly available.

A North Korean refugee named Jihyun Park describes an even worse situation in her home country, where many citizens work and live in labor camps. "North Korea is just an immense labor camp," Jihyun told me.

It's worth noting that in the United States, some prisons force their inmates to work, sometimes for nothing, sometimes for as little as two cents an hour, while the facilities profit off their labor. The prison industrial complex is alive and well in the West, too.

There are no rules in debt bondage, and that is true about slavery in general: It's a 100 percent criminal activity, after all. However, we can discern the business models if we look closely enough. Only by making sense of the various strategies and shapes of this monstrous industry will we find the path to eradicating it.

4

A Tattoo on Your Soul

Corruption and Impunity

Debt bondage is not limited to forced labor: It occurs in sex trafficking as well. It certainly happened to Marcela Loaiza, a Colombian woman who also had an immense debt to repay. Marcela is from Latin America and now lives in Las Vegas, where she has found a loving relationship. She is one of the very few survivors I've met who seems to have almost completely overcome the trauma of slavery, although, as she says so beautifully, it leaves "a tattoo on your soul."

After being trafficked she rebuilt her life and recovered enough, mentally and physically, to be able to fall in love, forge a trusting relationship, get married, and have two children. Marcela is my ray of hope in the dark world of slavery and vivid proof that one can build on the worst experiences and become a better person.

Like most survivors I know, she believes in God and says that He helped her come out of her trauma and showed her the light at the end of a long tunnel. She seems fulfilled and enjoys her life. This is partly because she started an anti-trafficking NGO in Colombia, the Fundación Marcela Loaiza, where they do excellent work to raise awareness of the issue and help survivors recover their dignity and reintegrate back into society with psychological treatment, access to jobs, and other services.

Marcela is petite and charming, with high cheekbones and a generous smile that makes her look younger than her forty-three years. The first time I met her, in 2014, she was already self-possessed and engaging—and also very funny. When we met again three years later, she brought me a copy of her book—a memoir of her experience of being trafficked by the Yakuza mafia in Japan—which, she tells me, has been a bestseller in Colombia.

That she was strong enough to write her story when she had just gotten married and started anew in the United States shows her bravery and determination.

Instead of hiding her past, she told her friends in Las Vegas and the whole world: This is what they did to me, transforming me into a prostitute, and this is who I am, a dignified human being who can look you straight in the eyes. One of the most brutal mafias in the world could not break her. She recovered from her trauma and overcame her shame—no mean feat for a survivor.

This is her story, in her own voice:

I was struggling economically. I was twenty-one years old and had been a single mother since I was sixteen. My daughter was born with health problems. I had two jobs at that time: I was a cashier in a supermarket during the week and, on the weekends, a dancer in a nightclub. I want to make clear that I was not table dancing, or pole-dancing. I was a professional dancer.

One day, a man approached me after my show and offered me a job. He said he was a manager and he could make me famous. "You are a great dancer, you are pretty. I am a celebrity and I will take you around the world as a dancer," he told me.

I said no, thank you, because anyway I didn't need a job. I had my normal life, with my two jobs, and things were fine. Several months later, my daughter got sick with an asthma attack that took her to the hospital. She had to stay for two weeks, and I stayed with her day and night, 24/7. So I lost both my jobs.

Unfortunately, I had kept the card from the guy who'd approached me in the nightclub, and I called him. When we met, he asked me why I had changed my mind and I told him about my daughter, losing my jobs, the hospital bill. He asked how much I owed, and when I said $500, he gave it to me immediately. No one else had helped me so willingly and quickly. I thought he was an angel.

He said he didn't have a job for me immediately, he had to look around, but he told me I was so talented and pretty that it would be easy for me to get a job. I was excited. I felt special. I felt like, wow . . . why did he choose me? I'm unique! This is fantastic.

In less than a week he found me a job, processed the documents, helped with my passport. And he gave me some advice: "Don't tell your family, don't tell your mother because maybe she will say no and stop your dream. And if you tell your friends, maybe one of them is prettier and better than you, and maybe I would give the chance to her instead."

I said, "No, no, please, please, I'm not going to tell anyone. Please give me the chance. I want to be famous." So, he used manipulation to control my mind. I did exactly what he told me. It felt like in an interview when you want a job: you just try to give the answers they want.

So, less than a week after that, he took me.

I lied to my mom. I said I was going to Bogota, the capital of Colombia, for a job. And that job would pay the medical bills for my daughter and everything. My mom agreed to take care of my daughter.

The night before I left, he said, "I will pick you up at five in the morning." And I asked, "Where am I going?" He answered, "Don't worry, I'll tell you in the morning."

So, in the morning, he gave me two thousand dollars, and the plane ticket. He said, "You are going to Japan."

I was excited. I had never even been on a plane before. I was thinking, "Oh my God, I'm going to be rich and famous." To be honest, I was not worried at all. I thought it was a big opportunity and wanted to take the chance.

I flew from Pereira to Bogota, to Amsterdam, to Tokyo, where I was trafficked by the Yakuza, the Japanese mafia.

In Tokyo, two guys were waiting for me at Narita airport, and also a Colombian woman. I was kind of afraid when I saw their faces because they looked a bit suspicious to me. It was the first time I'd felt afraid since I left my country.

So, I was scared, but also quite excited. Everything I saw was new; it was a completely new world to me. Immediately, the Colombian woman approached me and she spoke my language, so I felt comfortable again and very excited, very happy.

She was the sweetest person in the world. I'll never forget that moment. She said, "Oh, my sweetheart, you are so sweet. You are such a nice girl."

After all these years, I realize now what she was doing. Right there in the airport, with all these people walking by, she made me like her and feel safe. Then she looked at my body, from head to toe, and said, "You look fantastic. Oh my God. You are the prettiest princess. You are going to be so famous and make a lot of money." This made me feel very happy.

She took me to a house in Tokyo and said, "Let's go to sleep, you need to rest. You are probably very tired, and we'll talk about everything later."

I went to sleep. I don't remember how many hours I slept, but I remember she started kicking my legs. I was sleeping on a futon.

She said, "Get up! You didn't come here to sleep. You came here to work; let's talk about it." To which I answered, "Why do you talk to me like that? You are a different person. You were very nice at the airport and now you are treating me very different. What's wrong with you?"

"Well, you need to pay me my money back," she said. "What money are you talking about?" I asked. And she said, "The $500 you borrowed from me for your daughter's medical bills. And also, you need to pay for the plane ticket and everything, and on top of that you need to pay me for giving you this opportunity."

"Don't worry about it, I'm going to work hard and give you the money. I'll give you the $500," I said.

"No, you have to pay me $50,000." I asked her what she was talking about. "That is the price to pay for your freedom. If you want to leave, you need to pay me $50,000," she said.

I couldn't help crying, then I tried to go against her, and I put on a rebellious attitude. I said, "Maybe I'll call the police; maybe they'll help me go back to my country."

And I remember she gave me the phone and said, "Call them. Maybe they'll understand, maybe they'll help you get back to your country, but I don't know if you are going to make it in time for your daughter's funeral."

She meant they were going to kill my daughter. She said, "I want you to also remember I know where your mom works; I know where your brother goes; I know where your sister's high school is." I asked how she knew all this. Then I remembered that the nice guy in Pereira asked me so many questions, and I told him everything. I thought, oh my God, how stupid I was! I just put myself like a piece of meat on a big beautiful silver tray for these people.

I was crying. I said, "Why are you doing this to me?"

"Look," she said, "you're going to be a prostitute. As simple as that. You'll be nice, you'll work for me and nothing happens. So, you pay my money, you work, you work with one customer or twenty or thirty a day until you get me the money back and nothing happens here. Then you go, I go, and we never meet again."

So, I worked for eighteen months in all types of prostitution, in all different places—the streets, nightclubs, massage with a happy ending of course. I always joke about it now. Because some people say, "Massage? What kind of massage? Prostitution, really?" People always ask me, "Why did you never escape?" As if I could!

For the first ten days, she put me on the streets. Before the end of the ten days, she already had the second place arranged. She'd already talked to them. There is kind of a rotation of the prostitutes. So, everybody was waiting for the new one to come. Later, I had to do the lowest class of prostitution, the worst disgusting job. I mean, none of it was ever going to be nice, but this was the worst, where you have to walk naked on a transparent floor before being chosen by men looking up at you from below.

Every morning she picked me up and took all the money I'd earned. Well, not always, because in some nightclubs, you have to stay for ten days. You have a little backpack, that's all. And you are not allowed to go out. Never. Just work.

They never made me take drugs because I always did what they said. I was the most obedient of all. I was so afraid when I saw the older ones who took heroin. They injected them, they also gave them pills, and a special tea. I never knew what it was, but it was a weird tea. Everything they gave to them was really bad.

They made all the rebels take drugs. They had no right to say no: they made them take it no matter what. They would open the women's mouths by force. They would inject them, they would make them take it in any possible way.

I never took the drugs because I saw the older ones: they would beg for drugs. And, of course, they had to pay for them too. So, it's a double business for the mafia. The women are working extra to get access to the drugs. I saw that all the time. I said, Oh, God, please protect me from that. My only goal was to be reunited with my daughter, as soon as possible.

When I worked on the street, there would always be mafia guys waiting in a car. You were not allowed to take one step onto the street to start to work unless you had paid in advance. If I didn't pay in less than ten minutes, they would beat me, they would hit me until I learned my lesson and acted respectful in the streets. That is Japan.

So, I dealt with them for eighteen months until I paid all the money. Every night, in a notebook with the schedule, the manager would keep a record of what I paid. But she tried to make the amount I owed bigger every time. She would say, "You were late this week, so you owe extra dues to me now."

I got sick a couple of times, and she took me to the hospital and she paid the very expensive bills. Afterward, she asked me to repay in full.

During that time in Tokyo, I made friends with many women from many different countries, especially from Latin America— Colombia, Venezuela, Mexico—and also with a lot of Russians and Chinese.

In all these countries the trafficking is run basically like it's one mafia. So, the mafia controls the prostitution in a country and they cooperate with mafia in different countries. For example, in Colombia, a woman will have a connection with this big Japanese mafia and will offer girls to them.

I had to give the money I earned to the mafia and also to my direct manager. So, for example, I had to pay my manager the $50,000, but when she would take me to the night club for a week, I had to pay the night club to be able to work there, and that payment always came from me, not from her.

As a survivor, it never comes to an end, unfortunately. You know why? Because when I was a victim, they forced me to call friends and women I knew in Colombia to come join me because "it's a great business and it's a lot of money."

When my manager forced me to make those phone calls, she was right there listening beside me and she was telling me what to say, how to manipulate the girl on the phone. So, recovery is really hard and complicated because you feel so guilty to have done that to others.

The women I called, the ones who came, did exactly the same as I did. They stayed and they paid the money. You have to pay because if you don't you are killed. In my city of Pereira alone, we have had three different cases where women escaped and went back home where they were killed. It doesn't happen every time, though, because I saw one escape and they never got her.

Many of the traffickers have been victims of trafficking themselves. My manager, for one, was a victim fifteen years earlier. Of the $50,000 I gave her, she probably kept very little, as she had to give a lot to her bosses. The hierarchy is important in the mafia.

I remember she used to say she had four or five girls on her own. "These are my girls, my babies." And she also had part control of a few other ones, from her business friends.

This sounds weird, but for a while afterward I thought I had been very well treated, because she never beat me, she never hit me. She brainwashed me completely. But it seemed better than the ways of other managers, who would beat up their women. I thought, At least she doesn't hit me; at least I don't have these scars on my body.

But this is not totally true. I do have scars. In the end, it's still a trauma. Being trafficked is like having a tattoo on your soul. No one can see it, but it is always there. You know, when people see me now, with my good clothes and normal life, nobody can imagine how painful it was for us—the deep trauma.

I remember that every single day she would repeat to me, "You are a prostitute, that's what you are born for. Remember that. You are not allowed to do other things. You have to be a prostitute."

And she would add, "Just remember that if I kill you here right now, nobody is ever going to cry for you. Not even your mother.

She has probably forgotten you. And even your own child, because you are a prostitute."

And when I went back to Colombia after I escaped, I asked everybody for help. And nobody helped me. So, I thought, "She was right. Nobody cares for me." I tried to get my relationship with my family back, but it wasn't the same.

Not because my mother was against me, but because I felt so dirty; I felt no respect for myself. I didn't feel proud to be a mom, with all these scars I had. I felt I didn't want to hug my daughter because I was so disgusting.

Before I got psychological help, that's exactly how I felt. My mom would want to hug me, but I didn't want anybody to touch me. And I certainly didn't want to have sex. Ever.

When I met my husband, I was on vacation in Aruba with some friends. What made our relationship possible was that I was living in Colombia and he was living in the U.S.—he is American—and we didn't have physical contact. It was the perfect relationship for me. For two years, we had a relationship with no sex. We just e-mailed. He was very respectful, he didn't ask me for sexual pictures or anything. So, he started to build confidence in me about having a relationship with somebody.

But before that, I didn't want to talk to anyone. I didn't even want to touch my daughter.

My daughter is now twenty-two, and we have a great relationship. We talk about it. She says, "Yes, Mommy, I remember. I would come close to you and you would say no. And I wondered: Why is my mom like this? And now I understand all your trauma."

After I got home, when I was in my house and somebody would ring the door, oh my God, I would go hide under the table. My mom thought I was on drugs. She was like, "What the heck is wrong with you? Why are you running? What happened?"

Because even though my mom knew I'd been a prostitute in Japan, she didn't understand. My family, nobody understood what I went through. They would say, "Ok, prostitute, what's the big deal?"

They could not know the trauma, the shock. It was very painful for my family, for my siblings to understand what happened to me.

But let's go back to Japan. I had this kind of regular client. The managers were rotating us around, and clients would do the same because they knew the rotation. So, this client always looked for me. Even now, I'm still shocked that this guy kept coming to me, although he saw me crying every time. I would cry and say, "Don't do this to me. Please be gentle. Be nice."

It's only a ten minutes service, sometimes twenty, but it feels like three hours. It takes forever. And to me it's shocking that all these clients would come, even though we cried most of the time. They just didn't care about us crying. I think this is Japan; in other countries men would have paid more attention to these tears.

I kept crying and telling this guy that I had been kidnapped, and he would say, "No, you are not kidnapped." I'm not even sure what kind of words I used because I didn't speak Japanese or English. So, it was very hard for me to explain that I'd been kidnapped. But he would say, "You were not kidnapped; you don't have chains; and you don't have handcuffs. You are walking in the street. I see you in the nightclub. I see you in the massage parlor. So, how can you tell me you are kidnapped? Why do you lie to me? You just want to use me to get more money."

I drew on paper and showed him Colombia, and a little girl crying. I made little symbols for Colombia, Japan, force, money, a plane . . . . He finally believed me. He said, "Let's go make a plan. How can I help you to escape?" I had one more week until I was done paying off the $50,000.

And I was extremely scared that once I had made the last payment, she would sell me to another manager. I had seen this happen a few times.

So, he helped me. He hid a wig and a jacket in the McDonald's on the corner of Kurokuro Street, the main street where I worked in central Tokyo. I went in, put on the wig and jacket, and walked slowly away. The pimps were at the street corner, but they didn't see or recognize me. And as soon as I turned the corner, out of sight of the pimps, I ran as fast as I could.

The client had given me a map and money. Ironically, the Colombian Embassy was only three blocks away from where I was working for so many months. I didn't know that.

I went there and pounded on the door. When it opened, I explained what happened. I said "I'm a prostitute." And the man answered, "No, you are not a prostitute, you are a victim." And I said, "No, I'm a prostitute." And he said, "No, you are not, you are a victim." I cried, "You don't get it. You don't understand. I'm a prostitute. I'm coming from the streets."

And that was the moment when I realized that no, indeed, I was a victim. At the embassy, they promised me they were going to help and give me a lot of opportunities in Colombia if I reported the case.

So, I went back to Colombia and reported the case, I gave all the names—everything—to the police. But in less than three months, my case disappeared from the system. I went back to see the progress on the investigation and they said, "I don't know what you are talking about." They pretended that I was crazy.

I was very depressed when that happened. I went to the government office and asked, "You promised me psychological help. Where is it?" They said to come next week and they gave me a coffee, a glass of water. "Tell me your story with a camera and come back next week." And I said, "But I need help." I was so traumatized. And I was very depressed and paranoid the mafia would get me back.

The fact that Marcela never took the drugs that her captors pressed upon her—successfully circumventing one aspect of the sex-trafficking business model—is what saved her. If she had taken them, she would probably still be in Japan. Or she may well be dead.

Imagine being thrust into the terrifying situation in which she found herself at age twenty-one, in a country where she could not speak or read the language, doing what she was forced to do. Most of us would do anything to numb ourselves against such terror and pain. But she had the intelligence to understand that if she fell into taking drugs she would never see her daughter again, as drugs would have annihilated her will and been her final undoing. She remained strong in her resolve never to touch them. She stayed clean, and she finally got out and was reunited with her daughter and mother.

And she is thriving now, after years of more terrible experiences in Colombia, as we will see later.

Once again, it is survivors who teach us how the system of slavery functions today. In fact, what we learn from Marcela is the single most central and significant strategy of the business model: how corruption affords traffickers nearly complete impunity from the law.

First, there was the Japanese mafia, the Yakuza, which has strong links with the sex-trafficking operations in the city of Pereira and presumably all over Colombia. The mafia is not only dominant in Japan's underworld: crime bosses can also be seen at cocktail parties alongside the country's most prominent businesspeople and politicians. They seem to be allowed to carry out their business without much meddling by law enforcement.

Second, Marcela's case simply disappeared from the system in Colombia, within only three months after she reported it for investigation. The authorities pretended to have no idea what she was talking about, making clear that someone in the trafficking ring had a connection somewhere higher up in the government. That is a particularly Kafkaesque example, but this sort of corruption is endemic, not only in Colombia, but also in Europe and the United States—and, of course, in Asia. As a result, traffickers are almost never prosecuted. We always find the same business equation: low risk and high returns.

The challenges are similar all across the globe. In some cities in the United States, for instance, I have heard of complicity at surprisingly high levels: police, judges, and elected officials actively participating in sex trafficking, either as clients or, occasionally, as slaveholders themselves. Similar troubling collusion happens in the United Kingdom and Europe.

The fact that anti-slavery efforts are not organized on a global scale is a big part of what makes slavery much less risky than other organized crime. With such a minuscule risk of getting caught, the criminals involved in this business can operate with impunity, confident that law enforcement officials and prosecutors are not going to interfere.

Governments around the world spend a combined total of less than one billion dollars a year fighting slavery—and the United States spends the lion's share. Not even a billion, against an illegal, $150 billion industry! It's a drop in an ocean of corruption and greed.

As a result, the number of human-trafficking prosecutions worldwide is tiny compared to the 40 million people who are enslaved: In 2016 there were 14,897 cases. But it is improving steadily: in 2009, there were only 5,606 prosecutions.

Why has so much been done to tackle money laundering or even drug smuggling, and yet we are still so far behind when it comes to arresting and prosecuting people who destroy the lives of other human beings by enslaving them? Corruption is usually a big factor, but there are a number of other reasons, too.

To begin with, slavery is very difficult to prove. Traffickers work in the shadows, leave few traces of their illegal dealings, and use coded language to communicate and advertise. Like all of us, they also use the web to conduct their business. As Cyrus Vance puts it, "The Internet has become the twenty-first century crime scene," a place where you can post millions of ads, repeatedly sell children and adults, recruit escorts, and advertise all kind of jobs. Social media fuels the fast expansion of the industry. Law enforcement has been slow to adopt these same tools and analyze the data in order to track the traffickers. We will come back to this point in the chapter on solutions, because it is often by following the money that we can get to the slaveholders.

It's relatively easy to make bondage look like legal labor or like simple prostitution. Sometimes, victims are incorporated into a larger workforce. In brothels from Israel to Dubai, trafficked women and men are camouflaged among those who work freely, the difference being that the enslaved don't keep the money. This happens also in factories, mines, fishing crews, and so on all over the world.

There is also an enormous lack of awareness, even among prosecutors, that slavery exists in their own communities. I said it earlier, but it bears repeating: with such high levels of ignorance among the only people with the legal power to stop these crimes, many slaves go unrecognized as such and are either left to languish in horrifying circumstances or are arrested for prostitution and petty crimes, which increases their vulnerability.

Jennifer Kempton's experience reflects this problem. She and her NGO colleagues pointed out the systemic ignorance in cities and towns across Ohio. It begins with the police doing regular roundups of trafficking victims whom they see as prostitutes. Then they throw the women in jail—as prostitution is a crime in most of the United States.

Furthermore, most prosecutors do not have the skill set to pursue trafficking cases. And it is always difficult to prove force, fraud, or coercion—central to the definition of human trafficking—when you build a forced-labor case. It is easier to prosecute for money laundering, where you don't have to prove these kinds of practices, than for forced labor.

Finally, because of the lack of awareness at the top levels of government, very few resources are devoted to these cases, which are labor intensive.

This self-reinforcing cycle is very difficult to escape, even for prosecutors who see the situation clearly and want to penalize such odious crimes.

We can also see impunity in action via the experience of Sarah, the sex-trafficking survivor in the United Kingdom whom we met in the second chapter. Sarah remained in school throughout her ordeal. She had foster parents and met with social workers regularly, and yet no one saw what was happening to her, starting at age twelve and continuing for the next seven years. Every social-service provider assigned to her case failed to notice that she was exhausted and traumatized from spending her nights being sold by her slavers.

The most extraordinary example of the system turning a blind eye to her situation was on her class trip to France, during which her traffickers arranged for her to meet clients. None of the teachers supervising the trip noticed that she wasn't in her bed at night.

She speaks of the "system failure" that allowed a child to be exploited in this way for so long—and that allows her traffickers to remain free to this day. After her rescue, the British police began to build a case. Sarah told them all she knew and was prepared to testify in court. But when the main target of their investigation died, the case was dropped! Her traffickers still operate freely. As a result, Sarah remains in danger, and therefore she doesn't go by her real name when she speaks publicly.

Of course, there would be no slavery industry without demand, and anti-trafficking workers make the point that the clients—or "buyers of rape," to quote Jennifer Kempton—are generally immune from prosecution. This is often true even in child sex trafficking, with twelve- and thirteen-year-old victims, and in many cases even younger. As one specialist told me, "They never put the clients' names and pictures in the papers, they only put the victims' pictures out there." None of the men who paid Sarah's traffickers to have sex with her when she was a child were ever investigated.

But this could change. In February 2019, a coordinated raid against the sex-slave industry took place in Florida: After an eight-month investigation, the police and law enforcement dismantled a network of traffickers in massage parlors that were often brothels in disguise. Instead of arresting the women—mostly Chinese women lured to the United States to work as massage therapists in spas, then detained in the facilities and forced to perform sexual acts on clients seven days a week—they charged the traffickers and the men using these services, including the billionaire owner of the New England Patriots, Robert Kraft. His photo was all over the media.

Because Kraft is a celebrity, the story made big headlines all over the world, but what is really important in my view is that the police went after the traffickers and organized a long and detailed investigation, instead of just arresting the women for prostitution as they used to do. Law enforcement identified the clients and the women traffickers managing the victims before organizing the raids in the massage parlors. It was a proper rescue operation.

If sex trafficking is difficult to identify and prove, forced labor is still more challenging. Very few prosecutors have pursued forced-labor cases. In 2017, Cy Vance Jr. told me, "Neither the police nor any investigative agency has walked into our office where they have identified someone who is engaged in forced labor. Part of it is that none of the investigative agencies, to my knowledge, are actually focusing on that issue." So it follows that there is a serious lack of resources devoted to labor-trafficking cases.

This lack of resources is true at every level of law enforcement. In Columbus, Ohio, for instance, where sex trafficking is rampant, there is only a four-person police task force assigned to the problem. They only pursue about 10 percent of the cases reported to them. Anti-trafficking workers report that when they give evidence of trafficking to the regular police, they are met with indifference because the officers don't consider it part of their job. There is a special unit for that. In Columbus, as in so many other places, it is completely siloed off.

Prosecutors need a human being to come forward, or they need other kinds of evidence—like financial data—to show that slavery is occurring. But the victims have good reason to be reluctant: they take immense risks when they come forward, and law enforcement doesn't offer real protection.

Forced-labor traffickers keep their operations totally opaque, of course, which reinforces their impunity. Prosecuting a forced-labor case can take many years, as it is a complex crime to prove. Instead, prosecutors often charge traffickers with easily provable crimes such as smuggling or harboring illegal immigrants.

Not only are those charges much less serious than trafficking, but it means the victims themselves are considered to have committed a crime: they crossed a border illegally, they stayed in someone's house and worked illegally as a domestic, and so on.

All these reasons mean that enslaved people are often afraid to report their situations to the authorities. First and foremost, resounding in their ears are their masters' threats to hurt their families or loved ones if ever they speak to the police. That was why Marcela remained compliant and quiet. Likewise, we learned from Sarah that her traffickers threatened to kill her family and friends if she told anyone.

The problem is even bigger if the victim has been trafficked in another country: "For foreign nationals, one of the issues is [that] 'even if I came forward and you could protect me, how can you protect my family back home because I come from a small village and my traffickers come from the same village and everybody knows each other and they will torture my family.' That's a legitimate concern. As a local prosecutor, it is hard for us to protect their family," explains Karen Friedman Agnifilo, number two to Cy Vance in New York.

Threats of violence and death are more effective in sex trafficking than in forced labor. When Martina Vandenberg—a formidable lawyer in Washington who seeks compensation for survivors for all the years they were forced to work for no pay—has a forced-labor case, her clients are generally eager to talk to the authorities and to help prosecute their traffickers. They are much less eager in the case of sex trafficking: "If we want people to actually cooperate in these cases, then give them witness protection, give them money, give them something," says Vandenberg. "Don't just let them twist in the wind and then expect them to cooperate." Protection for recent victims is crucial to prosecuting trafficking cases, but so far, no government is providing even close to enough of it.

There are plenty of other trafficking techniques for avoiding prosecution. One frequent and effective one is making the victims complicit
in the crime, or having them commit other, ancillary crimes so they
won't go to the police for help. Forcing victims to recruit other women
and girls, as in the case of Marcela and many others I have met around
the world, is a powerful and effective way to incriminate them and
maintain their silence.

There can also be complicated relations and attachments between
the slaver and enslaved that prevent victims from coming forward or
cooperating. Very often, the trafficker will make the victim pregnant
and keep the baby to use as leverage against their "merchandise." A
woman in that situation is unlikely to testify against her trafficker.

Vance points to another way victims are often entangled with their
traffickers: psychological bonding. "We also see it in domestic violence,
we see it in elder abuse. It is difficult for people who were victimized
by people they know well, and love, and are dependent upon . . . . They
are scared to turn against them." Jennifer described her blindness to
her trafficker's true intentions, thanks to his successful grooming campaign. It took years, and his increasing brutality, for her to finally see
the situation clearly.

Mary Fischer, Director of Survivor's Ink, says this phenomenon of
trauma bonding works in modern slavery just as it does in domestic
violence "where a woman is in a terrible relationship with her husband,
getting beaten up all the time, but she still loves him. She's got a twisted
perception that this is the only love that she's worthy of, or that she's
going to get. She's got that love and loyalty for him; she's bonded to
him. And all the abuse does not negate that love. In fact, if anything,
it makes it stronger because she thinks: he wouldn't be so angry, he
wouldn't be so jealous if he didn't love me."

Even when a victim does come forward, prosecutors often have to rely
solely on that one person's testimony. But for trauma-related reasons,
victims and survivors often tell stories that change in terms of chronol-
ogy or other details, and that therefore don't hold up under scrutiny.

Every expert I spoke to about this problem believes that it must not be confused with lying. Rather, it has to do with how PTSD affects the memory. Victims frequently lose their sense of time sequence during their enslavement—which makes sense: They'd lived in a world of terror and hopelessness, with no opportunity to make decisions for themselves, with no possibility to take notes. Timelines, events, and facts can get so jumbled in their recollection that prosecutors either don't believe them, or they cannot follow the story sufficiently to put together a coherent case.

And we must never forget that many victims do not even realize that they are being trafficked, in part because their masters have systematically stripped away their sense of having any rights. When Marcela escaped the streets and made her way to the Colombian Embassy, she repeatedly told the man who opened the door that she was a prostitute, even after being told that she was in fact a victim. While she understood perfectly that what had been done to her was wrong, she still somehow felt it was also her fault.

An American anti-trafficking specialist I know reports similar stories. She's known many survivors who understood the reality of what had happened to them only after they received information about trafficking: "They would say: 'Oh that happened to me.' And I look at them and say, 'I know. But I can't tell you it happened to you. You have to understand that this happened to you.' Because most don't."

5

The Psychological Impact of Enslavement

Jennifer Kempton was one of those victims who didn't realize what was happening to her. As we saw earlier, her great love became her trafficker, and for years she didn't see the situation clearly, even though he had put her in the hands of the most violent gangs.

We left Jennifer in the middle of her suicide attempt in the basement of the crack house where she had been trafficked in Columbus, Ohio. It failed: the rope with which she tried to hang herself wasn't secured, and her feet eventually landed on the floor. At that point, she had been trafficked for six and a half years. It was a life-changing moment, though she still had difficult times ahead.

Here is more of her story as she told it to me:

> I hit the floor and I was so angry. You know, I can't even die to be put out of my misery. This is all I'm ever going to be—some worthless, crack-smoking, heroin-junkie whore, just a piece of meat; something to be used, abused. This is all I deserve.
>
> And that's when a voice came out of nowhere and said "I have a purpose for you and it's not to die in the basement of a crack house." And I had to sit down there and wrap my mind around what had just happened. It was quite an intense spiritual moment

for me, because I've never known anything about anything and I have never been shown any love or compassion. I never thought I could even have a purpose in my life. So, a lot of thinking and processing happened in the next two hours.

I eventually went upstairs and told them I was going out to make some money. Had I said anything different, I would not have been allowed to leave, and may not have lived.

What I really did was go get help. Again, I have to stress the lack of resources. Because I didn't have insurance, I couldn't go to the hospital. So, I went to a suicide crisis place. But they couldn't find placement for me right away because of the insurance situation. They were kind enough to offer to pay for a hotel until they could get me admitted somewhere, which they guaranteed was going to happen within a week.

But the hotel where they wanted to send me to was situated right down the street from my traffickers. I had to threaten suicide right there, on the suicide ward, so they didn't send me back to the devil. They agreed to put me in a different hotel and then sent me to a hospital that dealt with suicidal cases. Because of the severe rope burns around my neck, they had to admit me, whether I had insurance or not.

Eventually, I ended up in a civil living community and I just started rebuilding my life. It was difficult because I couldn't get a job. And I still can't to this day, even though I have founded a grassroots nonprofit, even though I can rise above the adversity I faced in my life, even though I am capable of all this, I can't get a simple job like running the cash register at McDonald's. Because I have a theft on my record for stealing two pairs of underwear from Sears when I was homeless and didn't have any underwear. My traffickers weren't providing it for me, so I had to steal.

I'm looked at as a criminal still.

I have gotten the human trafficking expungement, meaning that the authorities recognize that I was trafficked, but in Ohio that only clears charges of soliciting, loitering, and prostitution from your record. There is a new bill in progress which would add other things into the current expungement law: drug charges that come with trafficking, theft charges that also come with trafficking, charges of violence because you've beaten another girl up for your trafficker. They don't take these off your record in Ohio just yet, but a couple of states in the U.S. have passed an extended expungement law, and Ohio is in the process of following suit.

I've testified in front of the judiciary committee and now that the bill is going to the state legislature, I'm going there to testify as a proponent. It looks pretty promising.

So, I couldn't get a job, and it was a really hard time just surviving. Because I was not on drugs or drinking anymore, I was feeling the intensity of coping with my PTSD (post-traumatic stress disorder) and anxiety. Everything was a struggle. Recovery is just not easy at all. That's when the real work begins, when you hit the ground hard.

After several months, I finally got a small job. I was doing okay, though I was still trying to overcome many obstacles. But I had another chain of enslavement.

See, when the boyfriend was grooming me while we were dating, I designed this heart-shaped tattoo with a banner running through it and this banner was supposed to remain empty so that later in life I could put my kids' names in it. I got it on my back. However, he paid the tattoo guy to put his name in the banner. He explained it by saying, "Oh, baby, I just want to say how much I love you. How much I will always be there for you and how I will always have your back." But when he was trafficking me it turned into, "Babe, you can't go anywhere. I'm always right behind you. You can't leave."

Then that night when I came back from the hospital having
just found out I was pregnant, he thought he was losing his
grip on me, losing his control over me, because I had gone with
another trafficker for a week and a half. So, he took me to the
tattoo guy again and tattooed "property of Salem" (his name)
above my vagina.

When I got sold into the other traffickers' custody I was re-
branded again, because they were my new owners. "Greg" and
"Sid" were tattooed on my neck. I couldn't go to the bathroom,
I couldn't take a shower without seeing my traffickers' names. I
looked in the mirror and the reflection looking back at me was the
girl in that basement that night. The girl who could not even die
to escape her misery. I still felt like I could never be anything else.
All I could see was that girl, and it was all I could feel.

One day, I was talking about it with an advocate at the Salvation
Army, telling her how I couldn't wait to get rid of that "property
of" tattoo. She was like "wait, what? Property of?" It blew her
mind. Even as an advocate, she had never found anything like
this. She told a family member of hers, who asked how much it
would cost to cover that up. I said probably $200. And she said,
"It's yours. You can have it."

Well, I didn't spend six and a half years on the streets and not
have some hustle in me, right. So, I went to a tattoo artist who
was a friend of a friend and said, "Look, I only have $200 and I
know that's a stretch to do one cover up but I have these three
very dominant brands. One on my back that says my trafficker
will never leave. The 'property of' above my vagina. And Greg
and Sid on my neck, which I have to constantly explain to people
who ask me about it."

I told him the tattoos were constant reminders of what I was
trying to escape and forget. They were marks of ownership and
violence. I told him that if I could get them covered up, I'd be able
to hold my head high.

And he agreed to do it. First, we did the one on my neck, with Greg and Sid, because it was so visible. I covered it with a flower blooming out of darkness. That was really symbolic to me. But now I'm actually in the process of getting that removed completely, because it's still a huge identifier. I've cut off my hair and dyed it to try to change my look, to keep my safety first and foremost. And this tattoo is still like, hello, this is who I am. Laser removal takes a lot of time and money. It will take fourteen to sixteen sittings under a laser. There will be a little scarring but not much and all the ink will be gone. I want to do that.

While I was getting that first cover-up tattoo, I actually fell asleep—they recorded my snoring. In that moment, it brought me back to the dope houses and the street, and it reminded me of all my brothers and sisters, mostly sisters, who had been branded just like I was.

And that's when I knew what my purpose was: I had to pay forward this freedom and grace and mercy that had been so freely given to me. I had to help somebody else reclaim her body.

I thought I could help a couple of other survivors I knew to get their tattoos covered up. I started getting a presentation together, to ask a nonprofit organization if I could run my project under their umbrella so I could solicit donations in total legality.

I started doing research and I'm looking at thirteen-year-olds who had their eyelids tattooed with "Swab's House" because the trafficker's name was Swab; girls with dollar signs on their temples. There was a big buzz over in Madrid, Spain, because a bunch of pimps got busted who were tattooing barcodes on their girls. They were putting the traffickers' names all down their legs. One of them had a whole list of rules on her back, the rules she had to follow and obey her master. It was horrific.

I looked at all this branding and I thought: How is this not a bigger issue? We are branding human beings like cows and this is 2014. How is this even happening? So, this nonprofit said yes. Now, I not only had the ability to run my project, but I also became a board member of the organization. I hit the ground running and started sharing my story to raise money to pay for other people's cover-ups.

It seems like it took forever. But in reality I left that life as a victim in April 2013 and by February of 2014, I had started the organization. Not even one year!

It's been pretty amazing. It started as a small local thing, and we now offer services internationally. I helped somebody in the U.K. recently. She had "whore" carved into her leg by her mother when she was five. Her mother later trafficked her and every time the scarring would start to fade because she was growing, her mother would re-carve it again in her leg. And now she has a beautiful warrior going down her leg and whenever she looks at that scar, she gets to see the warrior. It is an amazing thing.

And in the process of this artistic work, we send the survivors out to eat wherever they want, we provide transportation, so they have the whole day just to celebrate reclaiming their bodies and just knowing how special they are, how much we value them for surviving.

So, we do the re-brandings, we do cover-ups of scars and tattoos. We also offer removal. We have found that most survivors want to cover them rather than remove them, because it is very empowering. I've heard them say, and I know for myself (though it may not be true for everybody) that it is very empowering to take this ugly, demoralizing mark of hatred and violence and turn it into something beautiful and symbolic. It's symbolic, I think, of survival itself. Turning these ashes into beauty.

But we have also started a couple removals. And to help with scars from violence we work with artists who are able to cover scar tissue, like cigarette burns and stuff. I still have my cigarette burns all over my legs because I don't use the organization's money for myself.

I also help others to do advocacy, education, and training. I get to train with Homeland Security. I get to train with a lot of amazing people, and I go into schools. I get to do prevention education and talk about the manipulation tactics of traffickers, victim identification, and so on.

With the kids I speak to in schools, I'm always age-appropriate. But for the most part, I'm brutally honest about how things in my childhood made me want to belong, how I had this need to fit in. How it started with a rape, and nobody believed me, and we didn't talk about it. I explain how I stuffed it down and started using recreational drugs. I talk about those emotional voids, the low self-esteem. I talk about the abuse, and how I felt.

I'll have a whole room of students, but maybe this group over here can identify with the low self-esteem, and maybe these two people can identify with the physical abuse, and these other ones can relate to the recreational drug use, and they can see how it starts as just having some fun, but then how it can get more serious. And they see what can happen. It's always well received.

Very recently, as I was doing my presentation, a girl stood up in the middle of the event and said, "Thank you for the courage to share your story, I'm going through this right now." She was being heavily groomed and pretty much ready to go.

Education saved her life. It's key.

I've had girls who've been trafficked, I've had girls and boys whose mothers have been trafficked, or their cousins or sisters. I've had an assortment of children that needed an outlet to talk about this stuff and need language put to it. They'll say, "Oh my gosh, my mom is a victim of trafficking. My mom is not a whore. Now I see this problem for what it really is. It's not just a choice to be a street prostitute, a drug addict; there are other factors." You feel the whole room shift. It goes from seeing these people in one way, to, "What can I do to help these people? Instead of criminal-izing them, I want to help them."

These children are not going to learn what they need to know from a textbook. Learning algebra or accounting is not going to save them from the danger right around the corner, or maybe even in their own house. They need to be taught real-life dangers and skills.

I know lots of parents and schools hesitate to bring in a pro-gram like mine because they don't want to subject the children to it. But you need to protect them by giving them the tools they need to recognize the danger that might be hiding in plain sight. I've been going into schools for two years now. It's been amazing.

We also get to work with Homeland Security. While I was out on the street, police officers I asked for help would say, "You are just pissed off because you didn't get paid." So, it's very satisfying to go to these police officers and say, "You looked at me like I was just a drug-addicted whore. That's all I was in your mind. But let me tell you, there's more behind that face on the corner than you see when you are driving by and thinking those thoughts. I want you to look at me and not see a drug-addicted whore, but a twelve-year-old girl who got raped, and didn't get believed, and was left behind. There's always something else you can see."

In the trainings I do at Homeland Security, I work with a Homeland Security officer, with a special agent, and also with someone from the state police. We're a tag team, and we go in and talk to law enforcement officers; we talk to social service work-ers. We offer them a continuing education credit so that they can come in and learn. And so, in this tag team: he talks about that deeper level, she talks about the state level, and I come in and talk about the reality of the life. We work together to give them the full perspective. And they always have a ton of questions because they had no idea.

How can you be a psychologist or a social worker, how can you work for child services and not know this? Child services were in my life from the time I was three years old—I was getting beaten so badly. They were in my life multiple times a year. Bruises and welts up and down my legs. They walked away and left me hanging there.

As a society, we teach our kids about stranger danger. But we are not looking at that neighbor who is a little overprotective of his daughter because he is molesting her and wants to keep her mouth shut. Or at that alcoholic mom who is taking her kids to soccer practice and not beating them, but she is abusing them psychologically. Or the cousin that comes over to the house once a year for vacation and that's when the little girl is getting nervous. We are not looking at the stuff that's right under our noses.

So, it's important that I tell child services the reality of what has happened to me, and the horror of how I was treated—how they could get their law enforcement officers to respond correctly in these crisis situations, to be survivor informed, trauma informed, compassion driven. Just because you have to do your job it does not mean that you cannot show compassion and decency. That doesn't happen enough in this world.

The next day, you know, maybe eventually down the road, they will open their eyes. So, if a little boy comes in saying, "No, I'm just being bad. I deserve this," because it's been imprinted in his head by his parents, maybe child services will see the bruises and understand what's really going on. It's really rewarding just to be able to go in there and teach them and share with them.

I'm also going to go back to college, for business management. I'm going for my associate's degree in applied science and then I am going on to get my bachelor's degree. I want to be able to help survivors who want to start nonprofits and social enterprises. Maybe people want to start selling their artwork, or maybe they want to get connected to people who will help them write their books.

In the process of managing my business at Survivor's Ink, I've made a lot of partners, a lot of networking connections. I've met a lot of amazing people. I continue to build upon this; I will be able to connect these survivors with resources, or to help them start their business at an affordable cost.

I want to use my degree to invest back into this. A lot of survivors go into counselling for drug and alcohol addiction, but I can't do those things. I've got enough trauma of my own and if I work directly with people, I will take that trauma on myself. I will feel their pain. What I can do is find resources. I can find connections. I am going to get that degree, and I will finally feel worthwhile. I feel like I deserve it.

It took me four years to feel that I will be successful. It's ridiculous that I was so conditioned to believe that I was always going to fail. Above that, I have been working out, getting myself physically together. That's been awesome. I've stepped back from a lot of things. I'm not spreading myself thin anymore—because I will, I will give everything I can to everybody else, and not give anything to myself because I don't feel like I deserve it.

I'm in that shift right now. Last night, in the hotel [in Washington, DC, where she spoke on a panel at the Trust Conference in April 2017], I didn't leave the room. I had a hot bubble bath and I lay there, and I got room service. I was doing some self-care. I told myself, "Jen, turn the phone off; you deserve some 'you' time. You don't have to solve someone else's problem all the time. . . . Just take your time for a minute."

So there has been a change in me. I am still helping other people, but I'm choosing my battles more wisely. I'm not running into every battle. I'm going to strengthen myself in my off time and then do battle.

Looking back at these last four years of recovery, I realize that when you escape trafficking, you just fall into another hell. You have to figure out employment, housing, your psychological issues as you work through the trauma, and the fact that you can't get a job because of your record. Plus, I am working to pay back child-support debt that built up while I was being trafficked. My child lives with his father and is now eighteen, so the debt isn't still growing. But I owe the state of Indiana, where they live, $20,000.

When I first started recovering, it was really hard to find a good therapist. There was this big pool of psychologists, therapists, trauma counsellors, but because I was on Medicaid I didn't have access to most of them. I wanted a female psychiatrist, and you have to find one with good knowledge of human trafficking. And you want someone you are comfortable with.

I did finally find her, about a year in. I actually got really lucky with my psychiatrist. I went to a trauma assistance program because a psychiatrist I met with soon after I left the street removed all the previous diagnoses, and correctly diagnosed me with PTSD. Finally. Thank God, he'd just come from the Veterans hospital, so he knew how to diagnose me and treat my problem. He told me that the best therapy I could get was no medication at all. It was group therapy that would help my anxiety and PTSD.

During that process, the group therapist referred me to the program supervisor, because they really did not know what to do with me. The supervisor also happened to be on the human trafficking task force, so she knew everything. It was a one-in-a-million chance. I could have been in any other program and the supervisor would not have known anything about trafficking. She helped me so much. I'm now trying to learn how to hold my head high and walk with it—and also grab some others on the way.

At the end of that conversation, I asked Jennifer if she believed in God. This was her answer:

I do. Yes, I absolutely know that God has been looking out for me. That's been a long battle. I was angry at Him. I cursed God out, and asked, "How could you let this happen? Where are you? You are so powerful, why is this happening, not just to me but to our children to this day?" But I believe He has been looking out for me.

Five weeks later, Jennifer died of an overdose. She never had the chance to go to college, or help survivors start their own businesses, or expand her educational work.

She had continued to struggle with her addiction, and had had a few relapses since she escaped, but she was so uplifted when I spoke to her a week or two after the conference that I just could not believe the news of her passing away. I was devastated. It was shocking, and heartbreaking.

For a while, I worried that speaking at the conference had triggered once again her post-traumatic stress disorder. Even though she often spoke publicly about her experiences, psychiatrists caution that recounting the original events can be re-traumatizing. So, I was somewhat relieved to hear later that the autopsy report definitively ruled her overdose an accident. Her best friend, Jess Graham, who discovered her immediately after her death, also confirmed that it was unintentional.

Jennifer's death shows clearly that the damage traffickers inflict on their victims is very long-lasting. "My therapy will not be done until the day I die," Jennifer had told me. "This is a lifelong process. I'm not trying to get over my past. I'm trying to learn how to hold my head high. And so that process is never going to end for me. I'm never going to be healed, probably not even close. But I'm okay with that. I was set apart for a reason. And I'm grateful for it." Such was her courage and optimism that she turned even her trauma into a source for strength.

Jennifer was so bright, driven, and accomplished. But, while she was working hard at her recovery, she still carried inside her the brutality and dehumanization of enslavement.

She went much too soon, just as she was going to receive the legal and financial help she desperately needed. I will not find peace until I make sure that what she has created with Survivor's Ink will continue the crucial work of helping victims whose bodies have been branded by their traffickers.

In the months after Jennifer's death, I frequently found myself searching for a reason for it. Why had she relapsed? She had apparently been thriving, and she had achieved so much. She had incorporated her NGO, Survivors' Ink; she was training Homeland Security, educating schoolchildren. She remained incredibly active and ambitious. At the conference, I'd introduced her to lawyers who could help her clear up her criminal records and cancel the $20,000 debt to the government.

I learned later, from one of her friends, that she was very inspired and uplifted when she got home from the conference. Up until two days before her death, her spirits were still high. It was unbearable to learn that she had been plunged back into a suffering so bleak that she returned to the drugs her traffickers had used to subjugate her.

Inevitably, this line of thinking led me to a big question: How do we truly help survivors recover and move forward with their lives?

The basic problem is that society leaves them in a huge hole. They receive vastly inadequate support when they get out of the terror of slavery. This is especially true for their psychological needs: They simply cannot recover in the short time period during which most governments will pay for rehabilitation. In the United Kingdom and most states in the United States, victims receive care for only forty-five days. They need a lot more: a place to live, identity papers if their traffickers kept them or moved them across borders, treatment for their addictions, access to so many services. But psychological treatment is obviously an essential first step in their recovery, and we fail to provide it sufficiently.

Speaking to this issue, the academic Kevin Bales told me about giving the keynote address at the largest conference of trauma specialists
several years ago. He told them, "You know so much about the trauma
of domestic-violence victims, you know torture victims, you know
military veterans and their specific traumas. But, do you know that
there are 40 million people in slavery and we know virtually nothing
about their trauma, unless you want to read a novel by Toni Morrison?"
Trying to lure some of the 300 people in attendance, he added, "There
are young psychiatrists here who could make a career of this, become
famous. Come and talk to me if you are interested." None of them approached him afterward.

Professor Cornelius Katona, medical director of the Helen Bamber
Foundation, cautions that, while therapy and other clinical treatments
can indeed help people recover from enslavement, it is an ongoing
process and the struggles are often lifelong. He compares recovery from
enslavement to recovery from addiction. "One of the tenets of the Al-
coholics and Narcotics Anonymous movements is that once someone's
an addict, they are always an addict and they are always one day away
from the next drink or the next dose of opioid. And it's a little bit the
same with victims of trafficking. They always wonder if there's something that will bring their symptoms back, even years after."

Cornelius Katona sees another parallel in Holocaust survivors.
"One of the things that emerges from the very long-term Holocaust
literature is how people who have managed to live apparently normal
lives and sort of bury their memories of the Holocaust, in old age it
comes back . . . as their cognitive process which forms their defenses
becomes less powerful."

It brought to my mind Simone Veil, the extraordinary and brave
French politician, who said to her sons, "The day I will die, I'll probably
be thinking of what happened to me in Auschwitz."

Katona also speaks of how addiction is common among survivors,
whether they developed the dependency during or after their enslavement. "We see people sometimes . . . in an unsupported and vulnerable

position. They may turn to drugs because drugs are the only way they find to alleviate their worsening mental symptoms. They have difficulties in accessing medical support, legal support, housing, whatever, but it's relatively easy to obtain drugs."

All of this speaks directly to Jennifer's life and death. Indeed, it echoes her own observation that she would never be healed, and her recovery would continue for the rest of her life.

Post-traumatic stress disorder is the most common, and perhaps the most difficult, psychological impact of enslavement. Judith Herman, a trauma specialist at Harvard, has done important work on complex PTSD. It manifests in many different ways, but a primary feature is a phenomenon of re-experiencing via intrusive thoughts, nightmares, flashbacks—all of which get triggered by reminders of the trauma, which might include a branding, a perfume, or even a purse, as I learned from Jennifer. She told me, "I don't like carrying a purse. It triggers me because I used to have my purse stolen by the other girls. I used to carry everything I owned in that purse. Maybe a little bit of eyeliner, or a small, travel-size brush. If I got lucky, I maybe had a toothbrush and a snack. Anything I could get. I hated it when they stole it. I cannot carry a purse anymore."

Shame and self-blame are prevalent among victims, as we could see with Marcela and Jennifer. Again and again, we see people who blame themselves in an attempt to find a reason for the inexplicable thing that has happened to them. Often accompanying the shame is the sense that they somehow deserve their enslavement. There is a complete loss of self-esteem and of the ability to forgive themselves or feel compassion for themselves.

Many survivors cannot build an intimate relationship, even years after their enslavement. Marcela told us that she spent two years e-mailing with her future husband before anything happened between them. The fact that he didn't ask her for anything for such a long period of time allowed her to build trust in him.

Ben Skinner says that most of the survivors he met in shelters in Europe were "really tough." And the reason for such toughness is "because if they weren't tough, they would be suicidal; they would fall apart. I think that makes it so much more difficult for them to recover and get a normal job and have a normal relationship and fall in love, because falling in love fundamentally means being vulnerable. [In] so many of these conversations I would have with survivors—even three, four, five years out—they would talk about the challenge of even the slightest bit of intimacy."

I was curious if specialists had seen differences in the psychological impact of sex trafficking versus forced labor. Evelyn Chumbow, the American woman I introduced earlier who was trafficked from Cameroon as a domestic slave at age nine, says that when you get labor-trafficking and sex-trafficking survivors in the same room, they have incredibly similar experiences in terms of feeling total betrayal, experiencing total helplessness and tremendous trauma. Some of this is due to the fact that a high percentage of labor-trafficking survivors are also raped.

One particularly confounding psychological result of slavery that I mentioned briefly in an earlier chapter is the impact it usually has on the victim's memory. I have myself observed that a survivor's story can change quite a bit from one telling to the next, especially when a year or two has passed, so that it seems not to add up. And of course, in court, these apparent discrepancies can play against the victim and in favor of the trafficker who can easily discredit their testimony.

Professor Katona notes, "Trauma has an effect on the ability to remember what was happening at the time and so people may have difficulty retrieving their traumatic memories and putting them into temporal context. If you think about the process of memory even in our everyday life, about being asked to recount something that happened a few days or a few weeks ago, it's very difficult to describe it in accurate detail and in context. And often you and your partner will not have the same memories of that incident you are speaking of. Imagine how it is to talk about something very, very traumatic, when remembering it makes one much more distressed. It's not entirely surprising that they don't remember it very well."

He points out another factor that sometimes compromises survivors' accounts: "They may be ashamed of what has happened to them and worried that if they tell everything that happened, they would be looked at with disgust."

There is an additional explanation for some of this memory confusion: Fear. Victims who have been told by their traffickers what to say to the authorities would still be afraid of retribution, and rightly so. People who were trafficked into a foreign country illegally and want to remain there after they're freed from enslavement may get all sorts of different advice from other asylum seekers about what to say in order to secure a visa. Or for someone only recently liberated from slavery—their trauma still fresh—who doesn't speak the language in which they're being questioned, it might well be difficult to tell the difference between an immigration officer, their lawyer, or a mental health specialist. People will say whatever they believe will keep them safe.

My own sense of it is that survivors have survived because of their capacity to adapt to the people they talk to, as survival is always about compromise. The ones who survive are the ones who can adapt best, who can accept compromise in the face of adversity.

As a lawyer who has dedicated her life to defending victims of trafficking, Martina Vandenberg has spent many hours talking to her clients, and she doesn't feel that they lie. "I have seen omissions," she says, "but usually when my clients are omitting something, it is to protect someone else, something like, 'This person helped me, but they made me promise that I would never tell that they helped me.' They are not going to throw that person under the bus."

Like Cornelius Katona, she raises the possibility that victims would be reluctant to recount every detail of their experience because of the shock and horror it might engender in listeners. Katona has noticed survivors not wanting to be viewed with disgust. Vandenberg sees it in more practical terms: "People are afraid that if they tell you every-thing that has happened, you won't be able to take it. And if you can't actually confront what they have survived, then you are not helpful to them. If you're listening to a client's account and you are crying, then you can't be useful."

As I've said, there is a terrible lack of psychological expertise on how to treat trafficking victims. But there are plenty of hopeful stories out there: Survivors do heal. So how do people recover? What are the treatments that have been found to help?

In his work with survivors, Professor Katona has learned that, in order for therapy to be helpful, people first need to be sufficiently stabilized both in their circumstances and in their acute mental symptoms. Psychological treatment must occur in the context of identifying and addressing all the survivor's needs—often some combination of general medical needs, protection, housing, welfare, and immigration stability. "If people are in unstable accommodation, if they have physical health problems that aren't being addressed, if they are in an immigration limbo, then those things can make it difficult to engage in any sort of psychological treatment," says Katona.

At the Helen Bamber Foundation, he and his team support survivors through a stabilization phase either before or as they begin trauma-focused work, which involves acknowledging that trauma and damage have occurred. As discussed, recounting one's painful experiences can be re-traumatizing, so clinicians have to proceed carefully.

I asked him about the outlook for survivors who do not have the good luck to receive or complete treatment; for most, therapy is simply too expensive. I wanted to know what issues they would face.

He replied that, for this reason, the Helen Bamber Foundation often uses time-limited treatments. Narrative exposure therapy is effective, and best known for its use in group treatment of refugees, though it can be done individually as well. Focused on helping survivors contextualize traumatic experiences within a coherent life story, this treatment usually lasts for six or eight months, or sixteen to twenty sessions.

Another form of treatment increasingly in favor is compassionate mind therapy, conducted in a group setting and usually lasting three to six months. Based on the notion that it is much easier to show compassion to other people than to oneself, the aim is to help them find empathy and understanding for themselves. As Katona describes it, "If other people show you compassion, it becomes a little bit easier to think about showing compassion to yourself, and feeling more deserving and less guilty, and beginning to rebuild self-esteem."

Then, after trauma-focused work, people need support in integrating into society. That phase is often less intensive but can take some time. Katona estimates that the total length of treatment is "very often well over a year, sometimes well over two or three years." And beyond that, some survivors need more intensive psychotherapy, sometimes for several years.

Of course, while trafficking victims everywhere experience post-traumatic stress disorder and suffer under the same symptoms, the therapeutic response has to be culturally appropriate. You can't give the same treatment to women in Africa or Southeast Asia that you give to children in India.

6

The Children of Bal Ashram

India is the land of paradoxes. The biggest democracy in the world hosts more than a third of the world's modern slaves, including millions of children.

And the children coming out of slavery—when they are lucky enough to be rescued—face exactly the same kind of PTSD as adults enslaved all over the world. Rebuilding trust in a child is no easy task and I have witnessed this extraordinary effort in Rajasthan.

We have already met the Nobel Peace Prize winner Kailash Satyarthi. The NGO he created thirty-five years ago, BBA (Bachpan Bachao Andolan, Hindi for the Save Childhood Movement), has rescued some 85,000 children from slavery, forced labor, and bonded labor, and it houses and treats some of them at two rehabilitation centers in Delhi and in Rajasthan, staffed almost exclusively by ex-slaves.

In May 2017, I spent three days at Bal Ashram, the Rajasthan center, with the rescued children and Kailash and his wife Sumedha, who is the ashram's director. It is a literal and figurative oasis in the middle of an almost barren desert: hundreds of trees of all sorts have been planted, one for each child educated there, and flowers bloom in spite of the heat. Most of the buildings are constructed with salvaged materials.

When I visited, there were sixty boys in residence (BBA does education and empowerment programs for girls, too), all of them jostling for the pleasure of jogging with Kailash when night settles and the 45°C days have come down to a much more palatable 35°C (still 95°F)!

Alpana Rawat, a counsellor at the ashram, is a smiley, warm, and charming woman who wears her saris with dignified grace and a lot of style. She seems very young, although she has been a practicing social worker for a number of years now. She sees the children immediately after their rescue and sometimes participates in the raids to free them. She sees the same PTSD symptoms over and over again.

All the children she treats have been mentally abused by their traffickers, says Alpana. "Mental trauma is big, and they are not able to open up themselves to anybody. They have a kind of fear in their mind, which their traffickers have put there; they say things like, 'If you open up your mouth to anybody except me, I will put you and your parents in jail.' Their goal is to frighten the children permanently. And it's easy: children are innocent. A seven-year-old boy doesn't know anything about the world."

When the children are rescued, they have generally not had any contact with their families for a long time, sometimes as long as six years. As far as they know, nobody has been looking for them, or even tried to communicate. Isolated from the world, they have interacted only with their traffickers and their fellow slaves for years.

In addition to the psychological trauma, they have also suffered physical abuse.

Alpana told me about a group of twenty-six children rescued from a garment factory in Delhi three months before my visit in 2017: "The kids were so sensitive. The owner and the trafficker were so cruel that they literally beat them with a hammer. They had children standing up for two hours if they did something wrong. One child is now around eight years old, but he was trafficked when he was four and still has huge problems. Another child could not even walk because he'd been continuously sitting in one place, working for twenty-two hours at a time, and sleeping in the same small spot. He had to hold onto things—furniture, stairs—to walk. Other children had lots of physical injuries all over their bodies. They were working in two rooms in a basement, never saw the light of day and the owner did not allow them to step out of the room—not even to the washrooms. And when they tried to nap, because they were working twenty-two hours straight, they were beaten with the hammer."

After being rescued, the children can't trust anyone. It calls to mind the two survivors Kailash told me about, brothers aged eight and ten, rescued five years ago from a sweatshop in Delhi. They were so traumatized that they refused to speak to anyone at the ashram, not even other children, for two weeks. And then one day they finally spoke to another survivor, asking, "Why are these people so kind to us? Do they want our eyes, or our kidneys?" They had never met someone caring, or even anyone with basic human decency.

"When the children are rescued, they are so suppressed. Their faces are full of fear. They are wondering where they are and who we are. During one rescue operation, one child thought I was there to harm him," said Alpana. It's heartbreaking, but it makes sense: How could young children know whom to trust after being treated so monstrously and believing themselves abandoned by their families?

I spoke with a few of the children—the ones who had already recuperated. All of them had been subject to unimaginable terror and abuse. One of them, Sanjeet, was trafficked from Bihar at eleven and put to work in a Vaseline factory in Delhi, where children would mix oil and wax together and, when it was sticky enough, put it in small containers to be sold to shops. They were working twenty-two hours a day. Sanjeet was rescued after one year, and he had been at Bal Ashram for a year when I met him. At thirteen, his dream is to become a grocer and to be able to eat everything he fancies.

Another boy, Emghaz, is sixteen now. He was trafficked at seven and put in a sweatshop where the children attached stars to saris while seated directly on the ground. After eighteen-hour work days, they slept right there on the ground, too. They were beaten all the time with iron bars and told their eyes would be poked out if they didn't work hard enough. Emghaz wants to become a singer or an engineer; he doesn't know which yet for sure.

Shivnat, now eighteen, was trapped in bonded agricultural labor with his father from age four. He was rescued by BBA at nine. He wants to be a doctor.

It's so heartening to see how all the children develop ambitions after beginning to recover and receive an education at the ashram. One of the children rescued from a mica mine spoke at our conference in 2014 and is now a serious student. When he was six, Manan Ansari was taken to the state of Jharkhand to collect the mineral that is used in all our cosmetics, in the paint on our cars, and in our phones. While working in the mine at the age of eight, he saw his best friend die right before his eyes. Rescued and educated by BBA, he is now at Delhi University where I met him again in December 2016. He has grown into a handsome and intelligent man.

We communicate by mail quite a bit and in his last note he told me he has started studying forensic science. He also wants to learn classical music. To me, it's a real miracle to see how this former child slave is now so confident in his future and expects so much from life, after a few years of education and treatment in a safe environment.

I asked Alpana how she and her colleagues manage to put these children back on their feet: What sorts of treatments do they use to help the boys recover after rescue?

She told me they begin with what they call "capacity-building sessions" with each child individually, partly to establish a rapport. They also conduct group sessions to explain very basic facts about the ashram: Why the children have been brought there, how the counsellors are there to help and not hurt them, and so forth.

The children are initially frightened of every adult they meet, because on top of having been enslaved for years, they went through
the trauma of the raid to rescue them. Kailash's team always conducts
these rescues with law enforcement, so the children are first brought
to the police station with their masters, usually with no explanation
they can understand. From there, they are brought to the ashram, and
many fear that they will be sent on to jail—and in their mind, jail is
worse than their masters.

"They have a lot of confusion and caution, so they will not even ask
where they are. These children don't know they have a right to education, to freedom, to play. They don't know they have the right to have
good food and good quality of life," Alpana said. Supplying them with
a basic understanding of their situation and their rights, and assuring
them that they are now safe, are absolutely essential before starting.

Every child who arrives at the ashram is immensely stressed, and some
display aggression in their anxiety. Art therapy is often the best way to get
the children to express themselves and address their experiences.

"What they draw at first is horrible. Children who have sad faces and
tears. Men with sticks or hammers, beating the children. One drew a
man like a demon, with horns. For their first drawings, they reach only
for the black pencils. But after one or two months, I repeat this therapy
and they make flowers, smiling faces, swings, in every kind of color."

Similar to how Professor Katona's team in the United Kingdom
simultaneously addresses all the survivors' needs—medical, psychological, safety, housing, legal—the ashram team tends to every need of
the children in their care, including physiotherapy (which most need
urgently after being abused in servitude) and a proper education.

Gradually, as the therapy sessions progress and the children begin
interacting with the staff and participating in activities, "they start
trusting us because they see that they have shelter and good food, they
have play time, yoga time, meditation time, TV time. Slowly, they start

to trust us. It can take a month or more. It all depends on the mental trauma he or she has."

Kailash and his team see many children recover. And in the safe and supportive environment of the ashram, some of them even thrive. One boy is studying engineering, another is building a career in yoga. They believe in themselves again. On the Saturday morning during my visit, a big party arrived: children from two villages nearby were joining us to meet Kailash. He is absolutely revered all around. Whenever he is in the ashram, they hold these meetings—each time with two of the very many villages where his team teaches children about their rights.

As I walked all around the ashram with Kailash during these three days, I was surprised to see everybody bend down to touch his feet with their hands. Hindus do that, I learned, to show respect to elders, and Satyarthi is certainly respected here. And among the ashram staff, he is utterly adored. That's partly thanks to the fact that he rescued most of them and helped them rebuild their lives.

It's remarkable to think that Kailash's anti-trafficking work began by chance. After becoming an electrical engineer, he decided he wanted to write instead and created a small magazine. He was working on it one day when a neighbor knocked on his door crying for help because his daughter had been taken by traffickers. Kailash didn't hesitate and went to help her. It was Kailash's first rescue. Since that day, he has never stopped. And he changed his family name to Satyarthi, which means Seeker of Truth.

When he appears in his impeccable white robes and greets the children assembled in the theater with all his warmth, kindness, and humor, they cheer for him as if he were a rock star. Then the show starts—but really, it is a conversation between Kailash and the children, who fight to tell him what has happened since they last met. One little boy explains that a father in his village wanted to marry off his twelve-year-old daughter, so all the children in the community came to him as a delegation to explain that if she were to get married, she would no longer go to school, she would have babies too early and damage her body, and she would never be able to have a decent job or educate her children well. The father listened, and no wedding happened.

It was, I must say, extraordinary to see that crowd of one hundred or so girls and boys, plus a few mothers, be so conscious about their rights. Another child, a beautiful girl who looked about thirteen, explained how she and the other girls lobbied the director of their school to build separate toilets for girls. And they won!

Kailash hugged each of the speakers and many other children, and they absolutely loved receiving such recognition from this Nobel Prize winner who meets so many important people around the world, including the Dalai Lama!

Throughout much of Rajasthan, BBA works to teach children their rights, and that model is replicated by many other NGOs all around India. Because once they know their rights and learn how not to fall prey to traffickers, children become difficult to enslave. Education is the way forward.

When I asked Kailash why there were so many slavers in India and if there was a historic reason for this, like the caste system—which was officially abolished in the constitution after the country gained independence in 1950—he said no. You find slavers in all strata of Indian society, he explained, even among the Dalit (the ex-untouchables) or among Muslims. The only exception, according to Kailash, is traditional bondage in rural areas, where the landlords are from a high caste and where the caste system was a major factor in bonded labor.

I asked Kailash what goes on inside the heads of Indian traffickers of human beings. He said that they often choose to traffic children because youngsters are powerless and relatively easy to control. His other answer was not surprising: greed drives them to it. In that, there is little difference among slavers all over the world.

7

In the Mind of a Trafficker

I had the extraordinary opportunity to speak at length with a trafficker's ex-wife in the United States, and she confirmed that greed and the need to control are central to every trafficker's motives. However, she also made clear that it's much more complex than that, with many factors at play.

Before he met Jennifer Kempton, the man who enslaved her got married at a young age to Jessica Graham, a very strong woman who gave me a lot of insight into the psychology of slavers. Jennifer became close friends with Jessica after she escaped slavery. She found comfort with a woman who knew so much about her tormentor. Jessica Graham, who now works at Survivor's Ink, has her own harrowing story, though she was never trafficked and she mostly got out of her dangerous situation.

We can estimate that if there are 40 million slaves in the world there are at least 5 million slaveholders. What goes on in the mind of someone who decides to transform another human being into a thing, take complete control over him or her, and sell him or her as a commodity? No trafficker has wanted to sit down with me to explain how he came to practice this crime, but Jessica's story and her observations fill in some of the gaps in our understanding.

Like Jennifer, Jessica is an extremely impressive and courageous young woman who puts herself in danger in order to rescue trafficking victims straight from the clutches of their masters in Columbus, Ohio. Tall and physically imposing, she approaches the local traffickers directly and fearlessly. When I spoke with her face-to-face, I could understand why these criminals find her intimidating.

Jessica's testimony is extremely rare. Most ex-wives of traffickers would live in terror of their former husbands, especially when children are involved, which is the case here. But she is not afraid of him—another sign of her incredible bravery.

In November 2017, a few months after Jennifer passed away, we talked at length about her and the man who sent her into hell for six and a half years, and then onto her drug overdose. Now well versed in the ways of sex traffickers, Jessica's observations about why and how they operate offer a useful profile of these people.

She notes that the two factors common to every trafficker she has ever met or heard of are greed and the need to control the people around them. In order to distance themselves enough from their victims, they must stop seeing them as human beings at all. They become objects and sources of revenue.

She paints a very clear picture of Jennifer's trafficker: A survivor of terrible childhood abuse at the hands of his own mother, as a young adult he gradually started to abuse others. Jessica's description shows how he developed survival mechanisms in response to his traumatic childhood, and how he came out of it alive. But the psychological toll was so enormous that he turned those same survival skills toward torturing others.

You will recall that the trafficker's name is Salem, and Jessica still knows him well.

In her own words:

Salem was raised by his mother in a rundown, hand-built shack on some property given to them by a pastor at the church near where they lived, in a very rural, woodsy area of Ohio.

Starting from when he was very little, his mother was sexually molesting him and his friends. When he was about six, child services got involved because he had been shooting a gun off and shot himself in the eye. This was the first time he tried to tell somebody about the abuse. His mother was in the room when he spoke to the social worker and I guess he was scared and didn't elaborate about who was sexually molesting him.

After the case worker left that day, his mother started to lock him in a dark, wet cellar dug out underneath the house. She would leave him down there for hours, to the point where he started hearing voices and thought there were people down there with him. This went on for years.

The man she said was his father lived down the road from them. When Salem turned thirteen, he went to live with him. Whether or not this man really was his father, we're not sure. But he saw that Salem was very intelligent, and he got him into school. He was not getting a proper education in the care of his mother, who was illiterate.

But this man had been in the war and he had severe PTSD. He'd have these mental attacks where he'd throw the table over, grab hold of Salem and toss him over, and tell him that people were coming to shoot them, and they needed to get their guns ready. But there was no one there. It was his PTSD.

So, this father figure, who was trying to give Salem a stable life, was unstable himself. Salem was with him until he turned sixteen. One day, he was looking for him in the woods and found him sitting on a tree stump. He had used a shotgun to shoot himself in the face. And Salem was the one who found him.

After that trauma, he and his friend left home and came to Columbus, the capital of Ohio. His friend was a little bit older than him. They got an apartment, and they got jobs. And that's when he started experimenting with different drugs.

When I met him, he was twenty-one, twenty-two. He was very charming, very nice, an absolute gentleman toward me. We'd been together only a couple of months when he asked me to move in with him, and I did. He had a job at Home Depot, a big home improvement store. He was the overnight manager. He went to work every day. It was a good job and he made good money.

And on the side, he was selling marijuana, which I didn't care about at the time. I was a teenager, everybody around us was smoking it. But I found out later on that he was also selling Ecstasy and cocaine, and that he was already using cocaine.

He was controlling over who my friends were, who came over to the house, where I went, what I was doing. He would come and visit me and say, "I just wanted to see how you were at work." I thought it was cute and he was doting.

Later on, I realized that it wasn't so cute, or because he loved me so much. He was just making sure where I was, and he wanted to see who I worked with. He was afraid that I was going to find someone else and leave.

He was a very jealous person. He didn't like anyone around me. He excluded me from my family, from most of my friends. I had two friends that stuck with me through all that and, at one point, he wouldn't even allow them around me.

And they didn't want to be around him. They didn't like him. They didn't like the way he treated me. I didn't see it. I thought he was just caring: that he cared about what I was doing and where I was going.

A month before I had our first daughter, he had a car accident, which left him in a wheelchair for a time. His doctor prescribed him 80 milligrams of the painkiller oxycodone multiple times a day and was giving him about 180 pills a month, every month. So, he started abusing it.

A week after I had my daughter, I went back to my job as a manager at a fast food restaurant, because he was not working—he was recovering from his car accident. The doctor eventually got in trouble for running what they call a pill mill: prescribing whatever medications just to get extra money. The doctor got shut down, and Salem's prescriptions stopped. He started acting very differently. He was out of his wheelchair by now. He started lying to me. Money would go missing from my wallet. He would be very reclusive. He didn't want me to know where he went or to see what he was doing. He would spend forty-five minutes in the bathroom. And he became very violent.

Around this time, people started telling me he was using heroin. I didn't believe them at first. I thought no, no, no, there is no way. We had seen heroin addicts, and he'd always said, "Oh, I'd never use a needle; I would never do those drugs. Why would somebody do that to themselves?" But now he would disappear and then he would come back and have these crazy looks on his face and he'd shout and yell. If I didn't do something exactly as he wanted, he would freak out.

I was now pregnant with our second child, and I told him I wanted to take my daughter and leave. He grabbed hold of me and threw me through the front door, then threw me on top of the car.

I left for a short period of time, and he called me crying and said, "Look, I have a confession. I have been using heroin. I want you to come back. I need our family together." He begged and pleaded for me to come back and help him stop the drugs.

So, I said, "Okay, if you want help, I'll help you." I've always been that type of person, if somebody asks for help, no matter what kind, I will help.

I moved back in with him, with a one year old and an infant, and things were okay for a week or so. And then I found needles in our furnace. I saw that the front of the furnace wasn't on right, so I went to fix it, and I found them. He'd taken the cover off of the furnace and put the needles and heroin inside. I called him at work—he was subcontracting. He didn't really have much of a job, he was doing small home improvement jobs here and there. I said, "When you come home, we need to sit down and have a talk." Well, when he came home, he brought two of his friends with him and I could tell he was high. I'd had my friend come pick my daughters up because I didn't know what he was going to do when I confronted him, and I wanted them safe.

He and his friends sat down on the couch. I said, "I told you I needed to talk to you." He said, "Anything you've got to say, you can say it in front of them." Later on, I found out he brought them so that if I tried to say anything to the police, they would take his side and say nothing happened.

We got into an argument and he started beating me and threw me through the door again. His friends sat there and did nothing. They watched TV.

I went back inside to get my daughters' things because I was leaving, and I was taking the girls. I grabbed their two diaper bags, and as I went to leave, he took hold of me again and threw me onto the coffee table. When I got back up, he was coming at me. I grabbed the legs of the coffee table and hit him with it and knocked him down. And that got me through the door.

That was the thing, Jennifer and I were both way stronger than him. But we didn't think we were. The coffee table was the nearest thing to me, and that was the only way to protect myself.

I went straight to the police station and filed a report. When the police went and talked to him, his two friends said I was the one beating him up and that he never touched me.

I went back to speak to the police officer the next day to finish my report, so I could file with the prosecutor's office, because I was going to get a restraining order. I had bruises on my arm. You could see his handprints from where he'd grabbed hold of me. And I had bruises on my face and my body. I showed the officer, and he said, "But I have two witnesses who say he never touched you." And I said, "I have the physical marks to prove it, that's the shape of his hand." So, we went to court.

I was granted a temporary restraining order against him, but they gave him visitation rights with my daughters. When he came to court, he had visible track marks from shooting heroin, still fresh and bloody. I told the judge about the drug use and she said it didn't matter, that was not her call. He was not allowed to take the girls anywhere, but he was allowed to come and see them without me present. He would show up high, falling all over the place.

Once, he even tried to take them. A woman showed up claiming to be a social worker. She showed me her name badge, she had all the documents for me to fill out. She said she was supervising his visits and that they would be at his house with her present. I thought it was legitimate, but it turned out she was a friend of Salem's; they did drugs together.

I got a call an hour later from a neighbor of his who said, "He is trying to run away with your kids." He did it to punish me and have control over me. I called the police, and also my uncle, who cornered Salem in a parking lot. His arms were bleeding from his track marks and he ran after my uncle with a hatchet. By then, he'd dropped the girls at a friend's house—somebody called me because they saw his van there. I went and got them. The next day, I went and talked to the judge. She still wouldn't put the girls on my restraining order, so I dropped it in order to stop his visitation rights.

He always gets his way when he walks into a court room. He knows how to clean himself up. He knows how to look nice. He knows how to pass a drug test. So, my biggest fear was that, even

if I told them about his severe heroin use, the court would always
side with him. They'd do a drug test, but he had passed all of his
previous drug tests. He could use drugs the day before and still
pass the test, he knows how to do it.

I asked Jess if he paid off the parole officers. She said, "Yes, that's
what he does. But when he got a new parole officer, he couldn't get his
way with that one. And he tested dirty, so he was thrown in jail."

Soon after I left him, he started working with a new dealer, a guy
named Troy. Troy had this girlfriend, Jennifer. I had met Jennifer
a few times. Troy got her working as a stripper. He kept her very
close to him. He was very abusive. She wanted away from it. She
wanted to work in child care. Troy was already controlling her life.
  Then Troy went to jail. Jennifer didn't know what to do. She
was left with the daughter she had from Troy. And here came Salem, and he was going to save her from all her problems. He was
going to give her a place to stay and take care of her.
  I tried to tell her, "You can't trust this guy. He did the same
thing to me. He was this wonderful person. He was going to take
care of me. He was going to do all these wonderful things. He
loved me." But Salem told her I was this crazy woman who didn't
want him to see his children.
  The way he was with Jennifer was a little bit different than he'd
been with me, because he had already progressed in using all
these drugs. He was seeing other men using women as their ticket
to make money. He was spending his money on drugs, and he
wanted to make more.
  He started dating Jennifer and he was taking care of everything
for her. He told her he would take care of her daughter and do
anything for them.
  And he could. If he really applied himself and he wasn't doing the drugs, at one point he could have been a great father.

But when he was on drugs, he was a totally different person. He didn't care about these kids, they were his ticket to getting what he needed. They were just leverage.

After a while, his money started running out, his drug habit started getting stronger. He ran his business into the ground and lost the house. He asked a drug friend of his, "How can you and your girlfriend afford this nice apartment and nice clothes, and you take as much drugs as me?" The guy told him he sold his girlfriend on Craigslist. The ads said massages, but they were actually escort appointments.

They were making all kinds of crazy money. They told him, "Salem, we can help you get Jennifer into this." So, he and Jennifer moved in with them.

This man and woman helped groom her. It wasn't until the woman took her to her first massage appointment—as they pulled up she told her, "You're going to do whatever he asks. He wants sexual favors, you're going to do it. Here's what you're going to charge."

Jennifer didn't want to do it and they fought in the car and she reminded Jennifer, "You know that your daughter is at my house with Salem and my boyfriend. And you want to take care of her, don't you? You want to see her, don't you? You're going to have to do this."

Salem always knew that whenever he wanted something from whoever he was with, he could use the children. Children were the easiest leverage he ever had in his life. He used them against me, he used them against his girlfriend before me, and he was using Jennifer's against her now.

About a year into his relationship with Jennifer, he came after me and my kids with a gun, so I finally got a restraining order with my daughters on it, too, for five years. I would hear things sometimes, rumors that he was selling Jennifer. But I didn't know what trafficking was at the time.

Two weeks after the restraining order was up, I got a phone call from a good friend of mine, who had been close with Salem when they were children. He said, "Salem got himself cleaned up. He's not with Jen. He wants to see you and the girls, to see how you're doing. The girls don't have to know who he is. He has been going to rehab and he's starting his life over." My friend thought it was all true. He was going to pick Salem up from rehab. He'd done a twenty-eight-day stay, so he'd had no drugs in his system for at least that long.

And I said, "Okay. If he is clean, we can meet. But I don't want anybody telling my girls who he is. I need to see for myself. And if at any point I decide that I don't think it's safe, it's over."

We sat with the girls and he talked to them. And he talked to me and painted a picture of Jennifer: a horrible person who stole from him and made up lies about him.

I didn't know Jennifer, I'd only met her a few times. So, here I'm thinking: Oh my gosh, this woman is crazy. But a part of me said, "He is lying to you."

We visited for half an hour, and afterward he asked if he could call to see how the girls were doing. I gave him my number and said, "Don't make me regret giving you my number because I will change it and you will never see or hear from us again." I protected these girls for so long. I will protect them for the rest of my life.

He said okay, no problem, no problem. And he called me two days later, crying. He said, "I miss my family. I want my family back." And I said, "We're no longer your family." I was smart enough not to fall for that. But I thought, if he wants to become active in their lives and learn about them, that's another thing. We could slowly reintroduce that.

And then I ran into a woman at a gas station. I can't remember her name. She said, "You're Salem's wife." I asked, "Who are you?" And she said, "It's not important. But I've heard you've let him see your girls. Keep them away. He's lying." I said, "How do

Jennifer Kempton in the office of Baker McKenzie in Washington, DC, where she told me about her life as a trafficked person and at Survivor's Ink in Ohio; April 24, 2017.

Marcela Loaiza in the office of Baker McKenzie in Washington, DC, where she told me about her life as a trafficked person in Tokyo and her recovery in Colombia and Las Vegas; April 24, 2017.

Deependra Giri onstage at the Trust Conference, Georgetown University, Washington, DC; April 25, 2017.

Kailash Satyarthi and Monique Villa, in Bal Ashram in Rajasthan, where he hosts children survivors of human trafficking; May 12, 2017.

Monique Villa and the children (all ex-slaves) of Bal Ashram in Rajasthan; May 12, 2017.

Jennifer Kempton speaking at the Trust Conference, Georgetown University, Washington, DC; April 25, 2017.

Monique Villa introducing Deependra Giri to the Thomson Reuters Foundation's team: Belinda Goldsmith, editor in chief, and Antonio Zappulla, COO; April 25, 2017.

you even know who I am?" And she said, "Just stay away from him." And I did.

About a month later, I was on Facebook and I got a friend suggestion, and it was for Jennifer. And I thought, I'm going to ask her what happened. I'm going to ask her how she's doing. I'd heard that she had gotten clean and was trying to do better with her life. So, I sent her a friend request and said, "No hard feelings. I know we didn't like each other in the past. But I've grown up a lot since then and I'm not a crazy teenager anymore. I just want to know if you're alright."

She messaged me back: "I'm really honored that you took the step to contact me and I want to say thank you. I'm doing really well. But for the sake of you and your daughters, I'd really like to talk to you. I have an event coming up. Can you come to it?"

And I said sure. And she gave me a little rundown of what had happened, and everything she told me fit with these rumors I'd been hearing all these years.

And she said, "I'm sure you've talked to him." And I said, "Oh, yeah. He said that you were this crazy woman and that you were trying to ruin his life." And she said, "Well, come to the event. Maybe you'll learn something."

It was one of the first speaking events she did for Survivor's Ink. It was in this little church. She said, "I can't believe you actually came. I didn't know if you'd believe me." And I said, "There was something about this woman I met at a gas station that is sticking at the back of my head, and she told me, 'Don't trust him, he's lying to you.' For some reason, I thought these lies have to do with you, Jennifer."

And she said, "I was not the only one. There were other women he trafficked." He would have a girl for a few days and then he would send her off to whatever gang. But he kept Jennifer for the longest.

Jennifer said, "I have a girl that I want you to meet and talk to." So, I met this girl and she told me, "Oh yeah, he was the nicest, sweetest person in the world. Most pimps don't let you have a place to sleep. They don't even let you inside. He let us come in. He let us sleep. He let us eat. He let us take a shower. But it all come at a price."

He was recruiting and grooming these women, then selling them to gangs. It was his ticket to making more money. He would have them for a short period of time just to get them to where they trusted him, and then he'd turn around and sell them to the gang members.

I confronted him, and he told me these were lies, that he had done some crazy stuff, but it was all behind him. I told him I didn't believe anything that came out of his mouth.

He said, "Well, I want to see my girls." And I said, "Well, they don't want to see you. They've seen you high as a kite."

At this point, Jessica told a painful story about how, a few months after they started becoming friends, Jennifer was tricked into being re-trafficked by a friend of Salem's. He asked her to come over to help him get off drugs, then locked her in his basement for six weeks, and got paid by the men who came to rape her.

Though they weren't close yet, Jessica felt a connection with Jennifer; they had begun telling each other of their experiences with Salem, and even in their early, tentative conversations, it was clear that he had controlled and abused them in similar ways.

So, when Jennifer went missing, Jessica felt compelled to find her, and went out searching for her every night for a month and a half, sometimes at four or five o'clock in the morning. Jennifer finally got free when the trafficker took an overdose and an ambulance and the police went to his house.

When Jennifer got out of that basement, she called me and said, "Hey, I'm in a safe house now. I've got all your messages on Facebook. Thanks for trying to find me. I just want you to know that I am okay." I said, "Can I take you out to dinner? I need to see for myself that you're alright."

So, we had dinner and we talked. I said, "Do you have every-thing you need at this safe house?" She said, "If I need more, I can get it." But I knew she would not and took her to the store and I bought her clothes, shampoo, a toothbrush, toothpaste —simple things that people wouldn't think she wouldn't have.

At first, she said, "I can't have you doing this. I don't have a way to pay you back." I said, "You don't need to. From here on, if you need help, you need to let me help you. You're the one who told me that you and I have been through the same kind of hell." I haven't been sold, but I've had other things happen to me. I added, "We need to stick together. Women need to learn how to stick together. We need to be an example."

So, she let me buy this stuff for her, and we went back to the safe house and sat on the couch and talked until 6:00 the next morn-ing, about all the things we had been through in our lives—the things that Salem had done to both of us, the threats he had made. And from that night on, every time she needed something, every time I needed something, we were always there for one another.

At a certain point, I wanted my daughters to know. I've never kept anything from them. Every time they have ever asked any questions, I have told them, when it came to Salem. I didn't lie about his drug use. Except I never told them that he never cared about them. I wanted them to learn that for themselves. I just kept everything factual.

My daughters had seen Jennifer on YouTube. The things we didn't want them to see, they found it themselves. So, they were very well versed on what human trafficking was and probably at that point knew more than I did.

Jessica then recounted a disturbing incident, which opened her daughters' eyes further still. One day, as they were preparing food for a party for Jennifer, Salem showed up very high in their front garden, blood seeping through his shirt from his track marks, and tried to talk to Abby, their twelve-year-old daughter. She came inside and asked Jessica to get him off their property. Their other daughter, Hailey, was eleven at the time, and hadn't yet learned the whole ugly truth about her father. She felt sorry for him and told her sister to leave him alone. Abby took her hand and said, "You need to understand that our father is a drug addict and a bad person. He's never cared about us and he's never going to."

They all went outside to put the food in the car and leave, and he approached saying he didn't want his daughters going to "that nasty whore's party."

And I said, "You have one minute to get off my property, out of my face, and away from me. Don't ever call Jennifer that again."

He said, "You need to stay away from her. She's a liar and a thief."

I told him she'd never done anything to me or the girls but love us and care about us, and that he needed to go away.

He said, "My girls aren't going. I'm taking them out of the car."

He turned toward my van and I grabbed him by his arm, right where he was bleeding. I stuck my thumb into his arm and I twisted it back around. I said, "You are going to get off my property because if I have to call the police, they will pick your body up off my ground. Do not go anywhere near those girls. They don't want anything to do with you. You're in no position to be near them. Stay away. You're nothing but a threat."

He said, "Ow, let go of my arm." I stuck my thumb in harder, and he screamed. I said, "You're going to leave now. Don't come back here." He left, saying he'd deal with me later.

My daughters and I got into the car, and Abby tells me thank you and Hailey's crying and she says, "I don't know why you should be so mean with him." And I answered, "You're going to have to learn for yourself. I can't tell you what you can and can't do when it comes to him because he is your father. But you're going to have to learn by yourself."

A month later, I was listening to Jennifer tell her story on the radio, and I didn't know until too late that my girls were sitting in the next room, listening. A few days after that, Jennifer was going to be on CNN, and she was going to use his name for the first time. She was very protective of my girls and had avoided using his name because she didn't want them to know. I said, "They already know. They've already done all their research. They know he's trafficking."

So, before she went on CNN, she asked my daughters for permission. Abby told her, "I want you to say his name. I want the world to know what he did to you. I want women to know they can't go near him, they can't trust him."

A couple of weeks after that, Abby came to me and said she'd gotten a friend request from Salem on Facebook. She asked, "What do I do?"

I said, "Well, what do you want to do? Do you want him to know what's going on in your life? Do you want to talk to him?" And she said no, she didn't want him seeing anything. So, she blocked him.

About three days later, she got a message from a man saying, "I know your dad, Salem. I have a son. I hear you're babysitting. Do you want to babysit him on the weekends? Here's a picture of him. Let me know. We can sit down with your dad and arrange it."

My daughter came to me and said, "Mom, something is not right here." I told Jennifer this guy's name and showed her his picture, and she recognized him immediately. He was the boyfriend of the girl who had groomed her when Salem first started trafficking her. And he did have a son, but he was almost twelve. So, he obviously didn't need Abby to babysit.

I messaged him from her phone, acting like my daughter, and asked, "How old is you son?" And he said, "He's a year and a half."

And I said, "Okay, how do I meet with you and my dad?" And he goes, "Well, I'll have your dad talk to you and we'll get a time together. You're just going to have to tell your mom that it's okay to go with your dad." I said okay.

I drove to Salem's house and he said he didn't know anything, he hadn't even talked to Danny—the guy's name.

I said, "You sent a friend request to your daughter and two days later this guy messages her. How does he know who she is? Nobody knows who your daughters are. I've kept them from everyone."

He kept saying, "I don't know anything about it." Then his phone rang, and I saw that it was Danny. I said, "Answer your phone." It had only been twenty minutes since I'd sent that message from my daughter's Facebook account saying, "Okay. Call my dad and we'll arrange this."

He goes, "We're in the middle of talking." I said, "You're going to answer your phone or I'm going to answer it." And he goes, "Well, nobody's touching my phone." I took the phone anyway. When I said hello, the guy immediately said, "Okay, okay, we can get your daughter." Then he said, "Who is this?"

I said, "You're busted. You come anywhere near my daughter, I'll kill you. Do you think you're going to traffic a twelve-year-old?" He said, "I don't know what you're talking about." And I said, "You haven't been messaging my daughter. You have been messaging me."

Jennifer and I went to the police, but since they hadn't actually trafficked my daughter, even with the evidence of their intent, the police said they couldn't do anything. That was the first time I understood the harsh reality. This is why we can't get anybody put in jail, because you have to catch them in the act. But how do you catch them in the act?

A couple of months after that, somebody set his house on fire. The police came to my door and said, "We know you've openly threatened to kill your husband. Was this you?"

I said, "No, I was at work. You can call my job. Do you think if I wanted to kill him, he'd still be walking today?" The cops said, "Well, you probably shouldn't say that." And I said, "Well, I'm telling you right now. For the protection of my daughters, if I thought he needed to die, he wouldn't be walking out of a fire."

They said okay and left. They didn't check with my boss or anything. In the end, they found out it was somebody that he had pissed off, probably from drugs, and he owed them money or something.

Several months later, I kept seeing Salem on my street. I asked him why and he said, "I live close to here," but he wouldn't tell me where. I was driving down the street one day with both my girls in the car and Hailey said, "Stop the car. There's his truck. There's Salem. That must be his house." It was maybe fifteen houses down from mine, on my street. I pulled up. Salem came over and said, "Oh, how are my girls doing?"

Hailey had learned the truth about him by now, and she looked at him and said, "Don't come up to this car. Don't talk to us. You don't know anything about us." He said, "Well, maybe I'll get to learn."

And Hailey said, "Is this the house you moved into?" He said yeah and asked if she wanted to see it. She said, "I don't want anything to do with your house."

Another day, in autumn of 2017, he came walking down the street toward my house. The kids and I were out in the front yard and I didn't want him coming near, so I drove up to him. And he went, "I just want to talk to you for a minute. Can you give me a ride to the ATM and we'll talk." I said sure because I wanted to hear what he had to say.

He got in, and my first question was, "For once in your life can you be honest with me? I know you're still on drugs. You're high right now. Are you still trafficking women?"

He looked at me and said, "I don't traffic women. I've never trafficked women. I help women." I asked what he meant and he said, "These girls out here, they don't have a place to stay, so I give them a place to stay and they give me money."

I said, "Well, how do they get the money?"

He said that's none of his business and started laughing. Then he changed the subject and started rambling about random things because he was high.

And all of a sudden, he looked at me and said, "I've just got three women. They're not minors, they are adults. They are in my house, but don't worry, Jess, I'm taking good care of them. I'm giving them food, I'm giving them showers, I'm giving them a place to stay. And I taught them how to make better money."

I said, "You are selling women out of your house?"

And he said, "No, I'm not selling them. They are selling themselves"

I said, "So, you have convinced these women to think they are selling themselves?" And he went, "I'm not the bad guy."

When I asked him if he realized this was illegal, he asked me to take him home. He realized he'd told me too much.

Soon after that, Salem asked Jessica for another ride, and again she said yes because she hoped to get him talking again and to record him this time. On October 11, 2017, she got him on tape discussing the three women he was currently trafficking. I heard the tape, and while it's often difficult to make out what he's saying because Jessica had to hide the device from him, he does talk about the women audibly.

Hearing his voice on the recording, it's clear that he was high during the conversation. That explains why he told Jessica about the women, and why he veered from ranting about how he "has three whores in his house" and he is "going to control everything from the black to the white," to a calmer, almost pleading tone as he insists that he is "taking care of them" and that "they are not in any danger."

I asked Jessica if she'd brought the recording to the police, and she said, "Yes. But they have to have physical proof. They don't want to hear anything on tape. They want to see it."

She went on to describe a situation in Columbus that is by now familiar to me because I've heard it described many times from different people all over the world: The local police are under-resourced, and basically uninterested in pursuing what they often perceive as prostitution. To be sure, charging people with trafficking is a huge challenge, beginning with the fact that in order to prove the crime, Jessica explained, "the trafficker has to be present. He has to be the one doing it. They have to physically catch him taking money from somebody."

Of course, traffickers are too smart to put themselves in that situation; transactions physically take place between client and victim, and the trafficker himself stays away, maintaining his impunity. And Salem continues to traffic women freely.

And we are not deep in Africa here, or in a remote part of Nepal, India, or Cambodia. We are in one of the wealthiest countries in the world, in a state capital 400 miles west of Washington, DC, and this was 2017. One might imagine that this kind of thing could happen only in a country with no rule of law.

But the America that Jennifer and Jess live in looks more like Dante's Inferno than like the American dream of so many immigrants.

It's easy to see how Salem has proceeded further and further down the trafficking path. We saw his earlier progress in his relationships with Jessica and Jennifer. As he became more and more addicted to heroin and crack, he couldn't maintain a regular job, so he grew more and more desperate and greedy. Even before trafficking Jennifer, he'd already had the need for control, evident in the way he'd tried to govern Jessica's life, telling her who she could see, isolating her from friends and family, monitoring her phone. When he stopped working, he relied on Jessica for income.

And then he did all the same things with Jennifer, though by then he had a bigger, darker purpose. In reality, it was a fairly small step from having an opportunistic, controlling relationship to going into trafficking. Jessica attributes it mainly to the drug abuse.

But it's also noteworthy that, even before Salem had the intention of trafficking women, his early behaviors in his relationship with Jessica were nearly identical to the grooming methods of the most seasoned traffickers: identifying vulnerable people, pampering them, and gaining their trust in order to control and exploit them. His abundant native charm is key to his success; he intentionally uses it to destroy women. It seems that approaching women in this way was intuitive—a natural outcome of his own trauma and of his desire for money and control.

His addiction was the final, definitive factor, intensifying his lack of compassion and his incapacity to love. It allowed him to objectify Jennifer further and further, until he saw her as no more than a thing from which he could profit.

Toward the end of the conversation, Jessica and her colleague Mary Fischer, director of Survivor's Ink, told me how men in their town are trafficked for sex just like women. I asked if Salem also trafficked men, and Jessica said no: "I think the reason he chooses women, and not men, is because of the complex that goes back to when he was abused by his mother. His need is to be in control of women, not men, because it was a woman who did that to him."

That wasn't the only time I was struck by Jessica's clear-eyed, even charitable, view of him; when she said he could have been a great father if he hadn't gotten into drugs, I was impressed that she could still see any potential for good in this man who had terrorized her and her daughters, the man who is responsible for Jennifer's death in the end.

He is a victim as well as a predator. He was a terribly abused little boy who grew into a damaged young man driven by greed, a need for control, and a bottomless emotional void that he tried to fill with drugs. As a victim of abuse himself, he developed effective methods to survive, which he then used against Jessica when he needed to—such as the time he brought his two friends home to be witnesses on his behalf when he knew he was going to get violent with her.

Likewise, his ability to present himself well in court in spite of his drug abuse is another survival skill. As Salem's addiction worsened, so did his controlling and abusive behavior, until he became the monster he is today.

That is how the cycle of violence is perpetuated. We see it happen over and over: Children are treated cruelly, and they grow up to treat others with further cruelty. Having received no love or kindness in childhood, Salem sought to fill that absence by exerting his power over other people. And he used drugs to make them obedient.

It takes an unusual person to break out of this cycle. Jessica and Jennifer—and many of the survivors I've met—are quite extraordinary in this regard: instead of allowing the abuse in their lives to turn them into perpetrators of further abuse, they've used it to cultivate their empathy for the suffering of other people and to offer support to those who urgently need it.

8

Limited Options

Like Jennifer and Jessica, Marcela Loaiza found redemption and healing by using her horrific experience to help other survivors. It has helped her recover her sense of self, and today she lives comfortably in her own skin.

When we left off Marcela's story, she had just learned that the police had "lost" her case files; a huge blow both psychologically and logistically. When her case disappeared, so did the government's promise of providing psychological treatment, leaving her, as she said, "paranoid and depressed." Beset by untreated PTSD, her self-image shattered, she came to believe in the way her trafficker had defined her. She describes what happened next:

> After the case disappeared, I went back home and thought, "Okay, Marcela, that woman [her trafficker in Japan] was right. You are born to be a prostitute." So, by my own choice, I became a prostitute in Colombia. I had tried to get other jobs but couldn't get one. The nightclub where I'd worked before had closed, and anyway I was too old for the new style of dance.
>
> One of my friends from Japan—we kept in touch—had a sister in Bogota who was an escort. So, I went to work in Bogota as

an escort. But I never had a pimp. And I thought it was great. I thought: Why did I go to Japan and have to make someone else so much money for so many months, when here I could do my own business? That was my mentality at the time. I did it for two years. I had again asked my mom to help me with my daughter while I was working in the capital city.

These are the funny little tricks. My mom already knew my past. And now I'd started to send a lot of money to her, but she never questioned it because she was benefitting. You know what I mean. I'm not against my mother. But as an advocate, I want to teach parents how important it is to question your kids about where their money comes from.

I sent money to my mom and my daughter. I paid for my daughter to go to a private bilingual school. I started to live in high class. I got an apartment. I made friends. I thought it was fantastic.

But I still had all my traumas, my problems, my monsters every night. Nobody knew about that.

After two years of this, one day I went to a bachelor party. They picked me up to drive me to the party, and there was a young girl there, probably younger than fifteen, she used cocaine and she almost died in the car. One of the guys said, "We have to get her out of the car, onto the street." And I said, "Don't do this, please." I saw my daughter's face in that little girl. I said, "Please give me money. I'm not going to involve you." He was a celebrity in Colombia. And he said, "I'll give you money, but never use my name."

So, he drove us to the hospital. I stayed with her. They did a stomach pump and everything, and she survived.

When she woke up, she said, "Why do you do this to me?" and I said, "What do you mean? I tried to help you." And she said, "No, I want to die. I want to kill myself." I asked why, and she said, "Because my mother is a prostitute and I hate it. I don't want my life."

It was like my daughter was talking to me, and I thought this is the end. I'm not going to do this anymore.

I talked to the girl, and I talked to her mom. She said thank you. They didn't know me or anything about my past. But that was a big lesson for me. I decided that I was not going to lose my daughter.

So, after that, I saved some money. I asked a few regular clients to give me some more money. I said, "I'm going to get out of this business. I want to be a regular person. I want to have a regular job." At first, they said, "You're lying. You just want some extra money to buy your Louis Vuitton, but you are going to keep doing this." I promised them that was not true, that I really wanted to stop.

Two of them believed me and gave me money. The other one did not.

And I went back home to Pereira. But every time I tried to do something right, something bad happened. I bought computers and started an internet café, but I got robbed, they stole my computers. So, I tried to start a business selling perfumes, but nobody paid me back. Later, I worked with Avon; then I tried magazine sales. But nothing worked.

One day I went in a church and I said, "Why? Why does everything I try go wrong'?" In the church, I met a nun. This was a miracle of God. He made me go to that church just when she was there.

We spoke. I told her my story, and she told me, "You are a victim of human trafficking. And because you never got psychological help, that's part of your trauma. That's why you went back to prostitution. You need help if you want to get better." She helped me find psychological help, and a sponsor, and my therapy went for three years.

And after that I never went back to prostitution, and there started to be a little light at the end of the tunnel. I got a job, I made money. I started to change my life. And everything became different, and I was so grateful.

She gave me a job in the church's school, in the cafeteria. I also asked for a scholarship, so I could study, and she said, "Okay, let's get you sewing classes." I said, "No, I don't like sewing. I don't see myself doing that." It's important to understand that all victims are not the same. You can't just give them what you want to give them, or what you think is good for them. Everybody is different. Maybe somebody loves to sew, but not me. How was I going to do something I didn't even like?

So, she gave me a scholarship to study English and merchandising and marketing. And I start to get involved with the government.

I switched my daughter from the high-class private school to the church school, which was a lower-class public school. The sister gave her the uniforms. It was a shock for my daughter to go from private school to public school, but she was happy, because she knew something had changed in her mom and she knew it was good, and she was happy in that school.

This sister was basically my angel. She helped me step-by-step and she changed my life. We still keep in touch. I told her that she is my second mother because I was born again.

But when I was in Japan, I was against God many times. I said, "Why are you doing this to me, if you exist? Why?" But now I believe from the bottom of my heart it was the greatest lesson of my life. I'm grateful because it made me stronger, a better person, a better mother, a better wife, a better daughter. It doesn't mean you have to have some struggle in your life to be a better person, but some people need it that way to realize how beautiful is life, to appreciate and be grateful for everything around you.

Before, I'd been against my mother because we lived in a poor neighborhood. And then when I was in Japan, I was starving for that neighborhood. I was starving for waking up in the morning and eating a simple egg my mother made.

So, that's why I say: some people need to understand how valuable life is, and love, and everyone around you. You don't need a materialistic life to be happy. Not at all.

The sister has tried to help many survivors but 75 percent don't finish the program and go back to prostitution. One of the problems is money. These kinds of programs give help, they try to give psychological help, but without money for training to get skills for jobs, it's difficult. The sister always said, "The difference between Marcela and the other victims was that she didn't care what job I wanted to give her." Because the only job she could give me at the school was in the cafeteria.

Going from my high-class life in Bogota, working with famous people, to the cafeteria—that was really difficult. But in a way, I felt so excited to work those eight hours. I made five dollars for eight hours of work. And those five dollars would somehow stretch. I'd buy food and good stuff and I'd still have some left.

When you work in prostitution, no matter how many thousands you have, it's never enough. But those five dollars—it was the most amazing moment when I enjoyed those five dollars. I felt so happy and grateful. And I was proud of myself. "I can do this. My daughter is okay, and she's proud of her mom." And now I can't even tell you how proud she is about her mom!

She is twenty-two now. She lives with me. She graduated from college last year with a major in biology and two minors—chemistry and criminal justice. And now she is working.

She wants to go to medical school and be a doctor. We will try to get her a scholarship. And she also volunteers at my organization, in Colombia and in the U.S. She is fantastic. I have two little daughters, and she helps me with them, too.

And I just had my eleventh wedding anniversary last month. I'm very happy.

When I met my husband, I was in the middle of getting psychological help. I didn't tell him about my past until I moved to the

States. I kept telling him, "I need to tell you something" but then I never talked about it.

I really wanted to marry this guy, but I wasn't going to tell him until after I was in the U.S. I didn't want to lose that opportunity. So, when he brought me over here, he proposed. And I told him my story. He cried like a baby. He said, "What are you talking about? What a horrible, terrible thing!" He was in total shock. He couldn't process it very well in the moment he learned.

I said, "Look, I really love you. I really want to get married. But I couldn't keep this to myself. I needed to tell you. I want to be honest with you. And if you really can deal with this, I'd love to stay with you, but if you cannot, please, do not deport me back to my country."

He joked, "You just want a green card?" And I said, "Of course, why do you think I stay with you?" We have a lot of humor in our relationship. Our close friends who know us well say, "I don't really know who the real hero is: you or him." And I think it's him.

He helped me build my confidence. When I told him that I wanted to publish a book, I was pregnant with our first baby. My daughter was thirteen. I thought it was the right moment to tell her the real story. She knew her mom had had something bad happen, but she didn't know the details.

I told my husband, "I need you to give me support because I need to tell Catherine about the past and I think it's the moment." And he said, "If that's what you want, I will be there next to you."

I told her, and she was shocked, and she cried. And I said, "Catherine, Jason, I'm going to publish a book. But if you guys tell me no, I won't do it. I'll put the book in the fire. It will be a closed chapter. But if you guys say yes, it's going to be a big journey, with big changes."

I'll never forget my daughter asking me, "Why do you want to do that?" She was still crying and crying. And I said, "Are you embarrassed about your mom?" She said, "No. Please answer my question." I said, "Because I want to help others."

My daughter stopped crying and said, "I will help you, Mom. If that's the reason, I will be next to you and I always want to help you." And my husband said the same.

I asked my husband, "Do you think your family can deal with this? I don't want to risk my family, my present, my future. I love your family and they love me but . . . ." And he said, "Honey, they already know, and they still love you. They've known since last year. So, it's not going to change anything, don't worry." So, they all understood and supported me. They agreed that I had to help others.

Soon after, in 2011, I created my legal foundation in Colombia, funded mostly by my family, my husband, and the company where I work here in the U.S. I also received an award from an NGO in Las Vegas, and with the $2000 they gave me, I helped twelve survivors I met through the sister. We paid for classes, transportation, and food for them. From there, some of them started their own small businesses.

One of them loved sewing and she wanted to mend clothes, but she didn't have a sewing machine. So, after I paid for her classes to improve her sewing skills, I asked on Facebook for a sewing machine for her, and somebody gave her one.

Another wanted to sell hot dogs. And somebody helped her, too, and now she supports herself that way. She says, "You have no idea how you changed my life. I have my own business and I don't depend on anyone." Now they believe in themselves. And just that small beginning helped these twelve women change their lives.

I went to the American Embassy in Bogota and I said, "Look, I'm your citizen. I love the U.S., and I'm grateful to it, and I'm going to do a workshop for all your employees here at the embassy, and in exchange you give me scholarships for English classes for these trafficking victims." The embassy gave scholarships to eight victims. Only three finished their program. But I was happy because I knew I made a difference with those three, and that those women will inspire others. I know raising money is important, but it's not the only solution.

In Colombia, there is so much corruption. That's why I went to the American Embassy and why I only work with the United Nations Office on Drugs and Crime (UNODC), because they don't depend on the Colombian government. The organizations that depend on the Colombian government are very corrupt.

One mayor called and offered money for my organization, but he told me that I'd have to give him back 65 percent of it. He said he'd give me $20,000 for the organization and I'd give him $13,000 back. My organization would only get $7,000. That's Colombia.

So, I try to change things and make a difference, but there are all these obstacles and sometimes I feel like I want to give up. It's really hard, because no matter what, it's my roots. But it's disgusting. It's very rare that somebody is honest. These people try to get money any way possible. It's really sad. It's the Colombian mentality and culture. But I also believe that in some way we can make a difference. Because if we let this happen, it will never change. And then what is the future for our kids and grandkids?

I've been working for four years with the UN's Blue Heart Campaign, which raises awareness worldwide to fight human trafficking. Also, we just started a new program, sponsored by the United Nations. This is the first time we've received funding. I think it was $30,000. We have victim groups and we are going to create a play with their stories, it will be produced after they are done with their psychological treatment. It's a beautiful program, I'm so proud of it.

Small groups like mine can make a difference when we network with other organizations and go into the communities affected by trafficking. Many NGOs, including mine, don't work in enough communities where the problem exists, in the small neighborhoods, and especially in the poor communities. We've just joined up with a program called Leaders Become Leaders. Twelve of the survivors we work with, who have just finished psychological treatment, are going to become leaders in this program.

I have an alliance with four universities in Colombia and one in Las Vegas. I went to them and said, "This is my book. This is my story. Can I work with your university? Can you give some scholarships to victims?" And they said, "Perfect! Let's go work together."

I work with victims in Las Vegas now, too. I have been doing more workshops there lately. I guarantee there are a lot of victims in Las Vegas. I think it's small pimps, small businesses. And I work with the police there, doing workshops with them in high schools.

Marcela's story fills me with hope for other survivors. She has forged a full, happy life for herself; she is able to love and trust her husband completely; she undertakes fulfilling anti-trafficking work that is growing in impact and scope. On top of all that, she has a lightness of heart that is hard to come by for any of us, much less for someone who has survived slavery. Much of that is no doubt due to her naturally upbeat outlook, her cool head under pressure, her generous nature, and her intelligence. But the impact of her three years of psychological treatment cannot be underestimated.

When her case file and the government's offer of support went missing, in the absence of psychological counselling, Marcela went back into prostitution. Desperate and hopeless, she had come to believe her trafficker—that she was good for nothing else. Once she met the sister and got into therapy, she was able to escape that false mind-set and see herself in a clearer and more positive light.

I asked Professor Katona about the outlook for survivors who do not have the good luck to receive or complete treatment; for most, therapy is simply too expensive. I wanted to know what issues they would face. Would they fall back into the same patterns, as Marcela did before she received treatment? He told me,

> One of the most important things is to realize that survivors continue to be vulnerable to the same things that have happened to them before. Many people we see at the Helen Bamber Foundation were trafficked from Albania. The classic story is of them having been controlled by a very patriarchal father and they then go away from home, usually to university, where they're befriended by a student boyfriend who pays them attention they've never had before because they've never been allowed to socialize. And that man takes control over them and then puts them into a situation of sexual exploitation.
>
> Having had that subjugation by their father and then much more extreme subjugation by the boyfriend, there is a terrible tendency to make the same choices again. Helping them to gain insight into that pattern, and to regain their ability to make independent and sensible and self-monitoring choices, is very important.

So how to help them do that? "One of the concepts we have encouraged is the need for not just recovery but sustained recovery," Katona explained. "People may improve quite substantially and be able to behave in superficially normal ways. But if they experience any further stress—like losing employment, losing accommodation, being moved, hearing bad news from home, having a challenge to their immigration status, developing a new health problem—any of those things may set them back into a much more symptomatic and vulnerable state."

His words made me think of Jennifer, of course—how her criminal record for stealing underwear while she was being trafficked made it all but impossible to get a job, meaning she faced real poverty and all the safety, housing, health, and psychological issues that accompany it. She was working to get the theft expunged and, indeed, to change the expungement laws in Ohio so other victims wouldn't run into the same issues in the future, but her record of petty theft remained a destabilizing factor until the day she died.

Unfortunately, criminal records are a very common problem among survivors, and they pose various hurdles to stability. Martina Vandenberg, the American lawyer who founded the Human Trafficking Pro Bono Legal Center, told me about survivors, with more than a hundred convictions on their records, whose traffickers have never been prosecuted. Poverty, joblessness, deportation, mental health conditions—all of these things can leave people desperate and with no option but to go back to bad situations.

Jennifer's death shows how addiction can also completely undermine survivors' recovery. When survivors are dealing with untreated trauma, the relapse rate back into drug use is very high because their PTSD is easily triggered. Drugs help them block out the traumatic memories.

I noted before how Marcela's refusal to take drugs while she was being trafficked played a big part in her ability to escape. It's clear that staying drug free also facilitated her recovery, because she never had to deal with relapses. Still, her untreated PTSD left her with such poor self-esteem that for a time she believed prostitution was the only way to support herself and her family.

Many factors can trigger survivors' PTSD. It might be one of the circumstances Katona listed: instability in terms of housing, health, immigration status, work, and so on. It might be the realistic fear of being found by their former trafficker.

Or it might be trauma bonding. Mary Fischer (the director of Survivor's Ink) explains, "[This] can be a big part of triggering people to relapse into drug use or dangerous behavior. It's one of the hardest things to break away from because they have such a connection to their abusers."

Mary has had some difficult experiences herself, and she describes how trauma bonding functions: "When you get triggered, you're put back in that mind frame. So, even if you've been out for twenty years,

all of a sudden, some guy comes along who reminds you of your trafficker, and you're attracted to him. Emotionally, you go back to that
place. When you are triggered, it takes anywhere from two days to two
weeks to be able to get yourself back to a place of, 'come on, I'm not that
person anymore. I am this person.'"

But people don't always manage to get themselves back to their new
mind-set, and to remain in recovery. Mary says, "All the guy has to do
is keep on triggering you to keep you right under his thumb. And then,
all of a sudden, you relapse, and might find yourself in the street again."
Life after trafficking is often precarious and fraught with danger. As
with a victim's initial recovery, sustained recovery also necessitates
steady and thorough psychological treatment.

The children at Kailash Satyarthi's ashram are likewise vulnerable
to falling back into slavery, as the staff is well aware. In these cases, it
usually has more to do with their parents than with the children themselves, who are too young to have true agency over their lives.

The ashram staff finds that parents often don't understand that their
child has been trafficked, and therefore they might unknowingly send
them into another dangerous situation. Once again, such decisions
are made out of desperation. Alpana Rawat told me, "The problem is
financial; there's a poverty problem."

She outlined how she and her fellow counsellors handle this issue:
"When the children come to the ashram, we approach their families
and give them counselling sessions. We don't want the children to be
trafficked again. What lasts is to motivate the children and the parents.
We try to make them understand that poverty is a vicious cycle and you
have to break it. If you were not able to get an education, at least you can
give that to your children. Because if your child is well educated, if your
child has a better quality of life, then he can recover and overcome."

PTSD and criminal records so restrict the pool of choices for survivors that leading lives free of misery and danger can be almost impossible—unless they receive a lot of support to help them stay on track.

Sometimes it doesn't work, as we saw with Jennifer: in spite of her courage and strength, she relapsed into drugs.

Jessica was with Jennifer the night before she overdosed, and she could tell Jennifer was not well. Jessica repeatedly asked her to stay at her place and talk, but Jennifer insisted she was tired and needed to go home and sleep.

The next morning, Jessica and Mary learned that Jennifer had left her house around midnight and had not been seen since. They knew this meant she was taking drugs. Using phone records and Facebook, they narrowed their search down to a few specific drug dens, but still looked for her all day with no luck.

By the time Jessica found her the next night, it was too late. Jennifer had smoked enough crack to shut down her heart, which happens gradually. The last person to see her alive recounted that Jennifer said she could no longer feel her legs and had wanted to leave. She was charging her phone to call Jessica and Mary to come get her.

Well aware of the signs of overdose, Jennifer most likely knew that she was dying.

9

Business Is Key—To the Problem and the Solution

Business is absolutely crucial in the fight against modern slavery. No big company in the world can claim to be slavery free, because forced labor exists somewhere along every global supply chain.

Millions of people work unpaid in factories, risk their lives on fishing boats, die in dilapidated mines, and are hidden so far down the supply chains of multinational companies that it is almost impossible to trace them. These include children as young as five or six. As I already noted, 25 percent of the slaves in the world are children.

They are today's forgotten people: unseen, unheard, and unprotected. Stripped of their humanity, they are locked in a cycle of exploitation while the appetite for cheaper clothes, more affordable phones, and mass-produced food continues to grow.

Let's go back to Deependra Giri's experience:

Unlike sex trafficking, the business model for forced labor does not rely on addicting victims to narcotics—indeed, drugged slaves wouldn't be able to function at their dangerous tasks in brick kilns or mica mines or fishing vessels or garment factories.

So, drugs were not a part of Deependra Giri's experience of being trafficked, though plenty of other obstacles were put in his way. We left Deependra when he was trapped in a labor camp in Qatar in

2009, receiving a fraction of his promised salary from the construction company where he worked as an office administrator. He was
not allowed to leave the country because he signed a contract saying
he would remain there for two years before taking any time off, and
in any case, the company had taken his passport. He had arrived in
Qatar one year earlier.

He was making ends meet for himself and his family—and keeping
his spirits up—by helping Andrew Gardner, a professor of anthropol-
ogy at the University of Puget Sound in the United States, secretly
document the working conditions of his fellow migrant workers. If the
company or the authorities had learned what Deependra was doing
on his day off each week, he would have been in serious peril. But the
danger didn't stop him.

> One day, Andrew offered to take me into one of the malls that
> are one of the main attractions in Qatar. Once before, I did try
> to get inside one, but the security wouldn't let me in. Europeans
> or Americans can go inside, but if we went in, their fancy mall
> would not look good because we are workers and we may spoil
> the beauty and luxury.
>
> I knew that everything there must be very expensive, so I
> thought I'd just do some window-shopping. Andrew took me
> inside and it was like, "Oh my god!" It was the fanciest mall I had
> ever seen, I would never have imagined it could exist. There was
> an artificial river, and the ceiling was covered with clouds that
> looked very real. It's hard to describe how beautiful it was. I do
> think that was the reason why they stopped me, afraid that people
> in the mall might have gotten angry and think: how dare this
> worker come here?
>
> I saw shops I had heard of before, big brands like H&M, Ameri-
> can Eagle, Louis Vuitton. I had never been to those places. And
> when I was going to go into the Louis Vuitton store, they stopped
> me. I said, "I'm so sorry, I didn't know. This is my first time."

Then I went to the biggest Swiss watch brand and was looking at a watch in the window. And I heard, "Go, go, go."

It looked very fancy from outside, but inside the people didn't know how to show respect. I know I cannot afford to buy these fancy things, but that is not the way you treat people. I'm happy that I'm not rich because I know how to treat people. I was just looking, and still they were treating me like an animal.

And by the way, quite a few of the goods sold in this shopping mall may have been made by slaves hidden deep in the supply chains of various companies.

Then Andrew took me out for dinner. It was very delicious, the first good dinner I'd had in a long time. So, I was very happy again, although I was also very sad because my family was far away back home in Nepal. I was desperate to hold my baby Aayushi, and talk to my parents and Sunita, my wife. And there were a lot of problems regarding my accommodation, and a lot of work pressure. But at the same time, I was very happy and I started to be very excited waiting for Thursday evenings when I would work with Andrew. I was so lucky to find him. If not for him, I would not be here today because he also introduced me to you.

I started working with him six or eight months after I arrived in Qatar and continued until I left. Andrew also introduced me to Mr. Giovanni, who was teaching in another city in Qatar and who needed help with his project. We would find construction laborers from Nepal, India, Bangladesh, Sudan, the Philippines—we located those who were not educated, who didn't speak English, who couldn't even read the traffic signs in Qatar because they were in Arabic and English. The plan was that every Friday, Giovanni and I would give them training, and then we would provide them with dinner and a training certificate. Giovanni had gotten a grant for the project from Vodafone.

Giovanni needed someone to assist him with the languages, so I worked with him for two months after I finished my mission with Andrew. We would go to the market trying to find people for the pilot project. He needed active people and I started to find Bangladeshis, Sri Lankans, Filipinos, Indians, Nepalese, Pakistanis.

At each training, Giovanni gave each of us a sun cap, a T-shirt, and a pen from Vodafone.

In my office in Samaiya—7 miles from Doha—things were getting more and more complicated in regards to the drivers who were now on strike.

To refresh your memory: Deependra had gotten involved in a dispute between the company and the drivers about their overtime pay. When the drivers started a strike, the company suspended all their pay and stopped giving them food.

It had now been five or six months that they were not getting their salary. Giovanni connected me with someone at the UN-HCR [United Nations High Commissioner for Refugees] and I explained the situation to him. He asked me to tell the drivers to gather all the documents they could and go see him.

The drivers went to see him, and he accompanied them to their embassies—the embassy of Nepal, the Indian embassy, the Bangladesh embassy. Then he went with them to the labor court and filed a case against the company for not paying the drivers their overtime. But at the same time, the company filed a case against them. The company was saying that as employees, these guys were misusing the company's petrol, selling it outside.

The court wanted proof of how much the company owed the drivers. They asked me to get them a hard copy of the salary sheet with the company stamp and signature and everything—the salary sheet that I'd made, and which the company had made me cancel. I said I could do it, but that they had to make sure not to get me in trouble. They were very grateful for my help.

The next day, I went into the office an hour or so early, before everyone else. I had the keys. I made a photocopy of the salary sheet and gave it to the drivers. I told them, "Please. I trust you guys and I am helping you. Because I am like you and one day I might be in trouble and you will help me." And they were happy.

They went to the labor court to fight the case. And after spending a lot of time there, and providing all these documents, and going back to the UNHCR, the court gave them an authorization letter saying that while their case was pending, they could go and work anywhere in Qatar. This is very rare.

So, they started to find other jobs, and I was so happy that at least they could earn some money. Finally, after a year, the court released an order to the CID—the police department that handles human rights cases—to fix the situation.

A CID Officer came to the office one day and when my manager saw him park his car out front, he told me, "I am busy and if anyone comes and asks where the manager is, you tell him he is not here, he is out of the country."

When the officer came in and asked, "Where is the manager?" I said, "He is out of the country."

"When is he coming back?"

"I don't know when, but he is not here."

He asked who I was, and I said I was the clerk. He asked what I knew about all these things and I said I didn't know anything, I only took care of the administration of the office.

The officer asked when he could come back. I gave him the manager's business card. The officer called my manager that night, and the next morning my manager asked, "Deependra, why did you give him my number? He was asking for your business card, how could I say I didn't know where your business card is?"

Then I asked what the officer had said. He said, "He is coming to meet me today."

I was so happy. The officer came, and he was shouting at my manager. They were talking in Arabic, so I could not understand much, but he was telling him he had to clear up all these issues. My manager just denied everything.

A few days after, the big boss of the police department came to the office. He told my manager, "You have by 6 p.m. today to provide the drivers with their salary for one year, their bonuses, and their airplane tickets. Otherwise you are going to suffer."

My manager had to prepare everything: the tickets, the salaries for one year, because for one year they had not received any money. And he had to go to the police department and pay the drivers in front of the police.

And so, in a week's time, they all went back home with their salaries and their bonuses.

For me, things were improving. I was working on Fridays and it was going well. And the company had put a generator in our building. So, for a while, we had electricity—which was extraordinary, although after a few months it broke down and we were back in the same situation. It was in May or June and that is the hottest time of the year. We had to sleep on the rooftop, but as our building was surrounded by cement factories, we woke up every morning covered in cement dust.

My co-workers asked me to talk to our manager, so I did. He scolded me: "Are you going to die if it is like this for one or two days?" I said, "No, we're not going to die but we need the basic facilities, at least. First, we need drinking water and water to take showers and cook food. And then, at some point, we need electricity" He said it was going to be arranged. I said, "Yeah, but you actually have to arrange it." I was firm with him and he got angry at me. And I said, "I have never done anything bad to you. I have always been very honest at my job. Why do you shout?"

It took two weeks to fix the problem. I sent an e-mail about it and one day I decided I would not go to the office. The manager got to the office and the first thing he asked was, "Where is Deependra?" All my co-workers had come to work. I had told them not to go: "You have to make the company feel how hard it is when you don't have water and a place to sleep. I have not taken a shower, I have not gotten rest, how can I work?"

When I got to the office the next day, one of the other staff gave me a letter and told me the manager had made him write it and I was supposed to sign it because I missed work yesterday. I asked if he had explained to the manager why I didn't come to the office, and he said no. I said, "If you write in the letter that I was absent without informing the manager, and the company is going to withhold one day of my salary, then you also have to mention the reason why I didn't come to the office, then I'll sign it. You can go to management and say Deependra refuses to sign it." And he said, "No, he is going to scold me." I told him the manager couldn't do anything to us.

So, he went, and I don't know what he said, but he came back with a smile and said, "Deependra, you don't have to sign that."

Later, my manager's boss, Jim, came for a visit from Syria and he wanted to talk to me. He said, "Deependra, how are things going? I have heard a few good things about you and a few bad things. Where should I start?" And, I told him, "Sir, let's start with the bad things and end with the good things, so I can leave your office smiling." And he said, "Oh, Deependra, why did you not come to the office that day? And you refused to sign the letter." And I explained the problems we had with our accommodations, and why I could not sign that letter. I told him we didn't have illegal demands. These were basic rights. And they couldn't even fulfill those. They were driving luxury cars, and we didn't even have electricity.

He was convinced. He said, "I think it's been almost two years, when are you planning to go on vacation?" He was changing the topic. I said I wanted to go the day after I completed the two years. And he said, "Okay, when you complete the two years I probably won't be here, so what you can do is make a postdated letter. I can sign it, I can approve it. Even if I'm not here, you can go; you can travel."

I was very happy. I made the letter and he signed it. He trusted me because I'd taught him how to operate his laptop, how to e-mail, how to make Excel spreadsheets. So sometimes he respected me. He told my manager, "Whenever Deependra wants to go, if I'm not here, let him go."

When I completed two years and told my manager I wanted to go to Nepal and showed him the letter his boss had signed, he said, "Okay, Deependra, I have to check with him. I need confirmation. I'll talk to him and let you know."

And he puts me off for six months, and then he said, "Deependra, we need someone to work in your absence." I said, "Sir, how can I find someone who knows how to operate Excel, make files and reports, and send e-mails? And how do I know he will be trustworthy? That will take a lot of time, I cannot do that." He said, "No, but you have to find someone." I said, "But, sir, I don't know anyone. How can I bring someone to you?"

I told him that instead of going for the two or three months' vacation I was allowed, I could take only two weeks holiday. So, he said, "Okay, let me think." I had already made up my mind that if I got a chance to go back home, I was never coming back to this hell.

After a week, he asked me to make a list of how much they owed me so far, with my bonuses and everything. He said, "We are very happy with your work, so we will give you two bonuses." I was so happy, I was going to get a lot of money.

But when everything was signed, he said, "We will withhold three months' salary and it will be paid to you once you return from home." I had zero money.

Again and again, Deependra was asked to sign documents: First by the extortionate moneylender, who called him back to sign a second, suffocating contract out of sight of lawyers or witnesses. And then by his managers at the company, who wrote and signed letters promising various things in order to gain Deependra's compliance in a given moment, only to change the rules or go back on their promises later. He later understood that this was to protect the company from any possible legal action. If questions were raised, they could always show these documents, even though the company didn't hold up its end of the agreement.

My manager said, "You purchase the ticket to go to Nepal and then we will see how we can help you." To purchase the ticket, I borrowed from a friend. I gave my manager a copy of my ticket and I was expecting him to pay for it, because the company was supposed to pay for the ticket after I completed two years. But he didn't offer.

The three months of salary were about 3,000 riyals ($825), and the two bonuses made it 5,000 ($1,375), and the ticket was 1,200 riyals ($330). So, they owed me 8,000 or 9,000 riyals. I had not a single penny in my pocket. I'd been planning to take my family to nice places, to take them out for lunch or dinner.

Then I asked my manager to give me my exit permit. He said ok, but that night I didn't sleep at all because I had to be at the airport early the next morning and I didn't have the exit permit in my hand.

I went to the airport still without the permit. I was very anxious, wondering how I could leave the country. Then a guy called me and said: "Where are you, I have your permit." He gave it to me and I was so happy, it was so much better than three months' salary.

I went home, and after two weeks my manager called me and said, "Deependra, let's book your ticket, when are you coming back?" And I said, "I'm sorry to say and at the same time I'm very glad to tell you that I'm not going to come back." He asked me,

"What about your salary?" And I answered very calmly: "This is a bonus from me to you."

Desperate as Deependra's family was for money, he gave up his last three months of pay in order not to have to return to Qatar.

But his debt bondage was not over. He still had to pay back the usurious loan that had sent him into forced labor in the first place. The 60 percent interest rate ensured that he would never be able to pay off the principal balance.

Soon, the need to make his debt payments while supporting his family drove Deependra to seek work overseas again. This time, though, he was equipped with know-how, and he successfully stayed out of the hands of traffickers.

First, he now knew what red flags to look for in advertisements and at recruiting agencies. He estimates that 95 percent of such agencies operating in Nepal are corrupt, like the one that sent him to Qatar. But on his second time around, he knew how to avoid the dodgy agencies, and he found one that gave legitimate work assignments. They offered him a job in Dubai—not in an office, but that was fine with Deependra.

Second, Deependra researched online. He learned about working conditions in Dubai in general. He looked at the company's website, the site location, and whatever other details he could find in order to get a feel for the situation.

Third, he simply asked questions. He had compatriots already working in Dubai freely, and they investigated the company and gave the green light.

So Deependra took the job, and it was clean: he was paid what they'd promised, he was given good accommodation and food, he was safe, and he could leave if he wanted to. Still, he was far from home and family and was there only because of his debt.

It was during this period that Deependra attended our second conference, in December 2013 in London, and the extraordinary happened, releasing him from his debt bondage.

Now Deependra runs an anti-trafficking NGO, the Safety First Foundation, in his region of the Himalayas. Starting such an organization was no easy task: He ran into corruption at every turn, with government officers asking for bribes to process his registration paperwork quickly. Everything you do in Nepal is tainted with fraud, he told me, so it took him about six months before his foundation finally got off the ground.

Then, in 2015, the earthquake struck, and Deependra and his wife and some friends turned their attention to the ensuing crisis. Through the foundation, they raised funds for food and medical supplies, which they brought to people in even more remote areas whose roads and trails had been rendered inaccessible by the earthquake. They also helped rebuild a school to assist the recovery of traumatized local children.

His NGO has also been instrumental in helping a few trafficked people come back from Qatar.

Deependra has now set up a center in his village, deep in the Himalayas, to help academics conduct research and collect data, just as he himself helped Andrew Gardner in Qatar all those years ago. Some of my friends in the trafficking world have used Deependra's invaluable services.

It is encouraging that more and more scholars are doing research on forced labor and that the media is shedding more light on the issue of slavery in the supply chains of big corporations. In the last two years, journalists have investigated the fishing industry in Thailand where slavery is endemic, the deaths of child slaves in the mica mines of India, football and slavery before the World Cup in Qatar, and child slaves in the chocolate industry in the Ivory Coast. They have also shown how hundreds of workers in manual car washes across Britain are lured from Eastern Europe and enslaved in debt bondage. It is the same with Vietnamese people enslaved in nail salons or hashish farms in the United Kingdom.

All these investigations have made headlines around the world, prompting not only awareness of the issue of modern slavery among consumers but also calls to action for corporations to clean their supply chains. Literally not a month goes by without the publication of one of these investigations. The Thomson Reuters Foundation that I lead has published a few of them and has trained journalists around the world how to cover the issue in their country. Every time a corporation gets media attention for wrongdoing in their production lines or forced labor in their industry, they react quickly. Nothing is worse for a corporation than the risk of seeing its brand damaged by bad practices and violations of human rights.

The next big shift for slavery will happen the day consumers decide not to buy frozen shrimp coming from Thailand or suspect countries unless they know slaves did not fish for those shrimp. I only buy fresh shrimp to avoid being an accomplice to the crime because in France, Italy, or the United Kingdom, fishermen are usually not enslaved. The shift will happen when consumers decide not to buy T-shirts unless they are sure the cotton was harvested using ethical labor practices. We are not yet there; far from it.

The mad appetite for fast fashion, whereby cheap clothes have to be produced in record time to satisfy ever-fickle consumer demand, seems to be never-ending and means the industry is always looking for cheaper, faster production. It is fascinating when you live in London to see that as soon as Kate Middleton or Meghan Markle wears a dress or carries a purse, the stock disappears immediately—so strong is the desire to feel like royalty!

But some consumer news is also positive. Recently a group of consumers in Massachusetts filed a class-action lawsuit against Nestle for "allegedly regularly importing cocoa beans from suppliers in the Ivory Coast using the worst forms of child labor as recognized by the UN, including dangerous child labor and the slave labor of trafficked children." The suit says that the consumers would not have purchased Nestle chocolate products had they known of these abuses. The outcome of the litigation remains to be seen, but it's encouraging to see such an innovative effort. To be fair to Nestle, I know the company had already started putting a lot of effort into cleaning its supply chain.

A specialist working for a big brand recently told me their research shows that consumers don't want to feel guilty when they shop. This means that any mention of slavery—even to say this product is slave free—is difficult if companies want to sell their products and not put consumers off.

We are just starting to understand that slavery happens everywhere in the world, right under our noses, and that it is not someone else's problem. I am optimistic that someday consumers will start to pay attention en masse. I don't know yet what will trigger it, but I am certainly working intensely on it.

Forty years ago, companies started to massively outsource the production of goods and services to countries where labor costs were cheaper. Mass consumption dragged down wages, and in some cases created the perfect conditions for forced labor to flourish.

Most companies are unaware when their suppliers use slave labor. Supply chains have become so complex that they are incredibly challenging to monitor. Many corporations that want to do the right thing are struggling to gain full visibility into the working conditions of those at the bottom of the chain. Their auditing systems are simply not adapted for it.

Take Apple. The giant tech company outsourced production to the huge Taiwanese company Foxconn, whose factories in mainland China were found to be rife with worker abuses. Working conditions were so awful that fourteen employees killed themselves, and another 150 threatened to commit mass suicide to protest their situation.

In 2012, the negative media coverage forced Apple to begin taking the labor practices of its suppliers very seriously. Since then, they have made substantive changes to their auditing processes and have dramatically increased the response when slavery and other abuses are uncovered. The company has spent millions of dollars compensating people forced to work for no pay and has enforced strict codes of conduct for their suppliers. Apple and its suppliers now work closely to stamp out exploitation—so much so that in November 2018, Apple won the Stop Slavery Award and was leading in all categories scrutinized. Apple is not slavery free, but it is strongly engaged in the right direction.

One NGO I have talked about has institutionalized the process of scrutiny in a very clever way: Transparentem, created by Ben Skinner in New York, conducts independent, on-the-ground investigations in several countries in Asia to document slavery. They don't initially go public with their findings—instead, they give them free of charge to the brands that have unscrupulous suppliers.

Once alerted, the company is given time to address the issues. If this doesn't happen, Transparentem will share its findings with the corporation's board members. If nothing happens even then, they can go to the media. Ben is a former reporter and this innovative method could only have been born in a journalist's mind. For full disclosure, please note that I am a director of Transparentem.

In 2017, the organization investigated several Bangladeshi tanneries used in the supply chains of Western companies, including Kate Spade, Clarks, and Michael Kors. Most of the implicated brands immediately took action. Even the high-end American handbag brand Coach—which initially denied the reports—finally spoke with their suppliers to make sure they would change their practices and stop exploiting workers.

But what has really triggered some progress in the corporate sector is the introduction of new legislation. After the California law that led the way, the U.K. Modern Slavery Act of 2015 requires companies with a turnover of more than £36 million to make public what they are doing to address forced labor in their supply chains. It's a beginning; of course, more remains to be done to give the law the teeth it needs. As it stands, there is no penalty and companies could simply write on their websites that they are not doing anything wrong at all without getting any penalty.

In 2017, the French Parliament adopted a similar law, though it focuses on the size of companies instead of on the level of profit. Only 150 businesses will be affected by the new rules in France. Australia also passed an anti-slavery bill in 2018, and the law goes further than in the United Kingdom, as it sets out what the report must contain and the consequences if businesses don't comply. The Netherlands is also passing a new law.

While legislation puts the issue on the radar of CEOs and boards of big corporations, which is important, it won't put an end to slavery. The problem with laws is that they have to be enforced. India, for instance, has many laws related to trafficking or bonded labor—the latter was abolished in 1976—but they are rarely enforced.

Indeed, India still has a third of the slaves in the world.

The real impact starts with cross-sector collaboration and shared expertise; with businesses, government, and civil society working together. We are seeing this happen more and more. No company can attack this issue alone, and they are getting smarter about collaborating with other retailers, suppliers, processors, and NGOs to identify risks of forced labor and to train suppliers.

The Responsible Business Alliance, a coalition of businesses working in the electronics industry, has committed to supporting the rights of workers and communities linked to their supply chains. The Better Cotton Initiative, a global cotton sustainability program, is uniting everyone from farmers to fashion brands in raising the standards of global cotton production. The goal is to improve working conditions, have a lower environmental impact, and strengthen the sector's competitiveness. And this is happening across many other industries.

Given the vast, complex, and multilayered nature of global supply chains, there is no doubt that combining forces is necessary.

I love the story Nicholas Kristoff, the *New York Times* columnist, told at one of my events. He was investigating the website Backpage .com, where women and children were being trafficked on the Internet, and discovered that Goldman Sachs had a 16 percent share of its parent company. He went to the bank with this information and asked if they knew they were invested in a website that is complicit in human trafficking. Horrified, Goldman Sachs quickly divested all its shares. To me, that is a real pity because Goldman Sachs could have used its power as a major investor to try and force Backpage.com to stop running advertisements for traffickers.

Investors and big funds, especially national funds, should also take their share of responsibility and pay attention to forced labor before investing in companies, in the same way they do regarding money laundering and corruption. There is movement on this front, with investor groups beginning to marshal their forces to battle slavery. In 2018, Humanity United, a foundation created by eBay founder Pierre Omidyar and his wife, Pam Omidyar, started a new fund to invest in young technology companies that fight trafficking in corporate supply chains. Backed by the Walt Disney Company, the Walmart Foundation, the C&A Foundation, and several impact investors, the fund has raised $23 million to direct into four investment themes: product traceability, worker engagement, risk assessment, and ethical recruiting tools.

In 2012, I started the Trust Women Conference—now called Trust Conference—in an effort to bring together the many different players, local and global, in the fight against slavery, so they can get to know each other, connect, coordinate, brainstorm, partner, and, in the end, take real action. We act together, not individually.

And we quickly started to have an impact: the Trust Conference is now the biggest anti-trafficking forum in the world. If we want to win the fight, we need government, business, investors, shareholders, and NGOs on the front lines. We need media, consumers, and, of course, survivors to act. We get all of these different actors in a room together and we decide which actions we will launch.

In 2016, the great and visionary artist Anish Kapoor created with me the Stop Slavery Award to honor corporations that are best in class in trying to clean their supply chains of forced labor. The award itself is a beautiful sculpture conceived by Anish. Candidate companies have to fill out an extensive questionnaire. We give several awards each year, and past recipients include Adidas, the overall winner, followed by Hewlett Packard Enterprise, Intel, C&A, NXP Semiconductors, and the Co-op Group. Apple won in 2018, followed by Unilever for the leading role of its CEO Paul Polman in the fight against forced labor, although the jury noted Unilever has a lot more to do to get clean.

All the winners told me that receiving the award has been a fantastic morale booster for their staff: employees are proud to work at a place recognized for its ethical practices.

It's worth noting that most of the candidates had some kind of media attention for wrongdoing before starting to address the issue of slavery seriously. Many big corporations were candidates in the first three years and this demonstrates that they are no longer afraid to be associated with the word "slavery." This, for me, represents huge progress.

Yet companies still don't want to advertise their anti-slavery efforts because they're afraid of making their customers feel guilty when they shop and putting them off of their brand. We know, though, that many solutions can only come from consumers. One day they will say, "Enough is enough!"—just as in February 2018, when a groundswell of young people in the United States decided abruptly, after yet another mass killing in a school, that enough was enough. It was time to go and fight the gun lobby and make their voices heard far and wide.

When consumers around the world realize that they can no longer be accomplices to the crime of slavery, it will become much easier to find solutions.

10

Solutions

From Individuals to Cross-Sector Engagement, Worldwide

For years, the human-trafficking industry has grown, hidden from sight. It's only very recently that people are beginning to understand that this atrocity exists in every country on earth. As we have seen, no big corporations can say, "We are slavery free," and all of us, as consumers, have most likely bought goods tainted by slavery.

I am convinced that knowledge leads to action, and I think that we have progressed considerably in awareness of the issue, essentially thanks to the media—investigative journalism is not dead!

States can no longer look away from the problem or say, "We don't have slaves in our country." Corporations can no longer ignore the risk of forced labor in their supply chains, in part because the laws now force them toward more transparency.

These are significant advances but we need many more. I am often asked, "What can I do to help stop slavery?"

Here are a few tips. All of them start with being an informed consumer: we can absolutely change the ways we look at things.

These are things we can do—every day:

ASK QUESTIONS

- Ask the sales people in jewelry shops if they know where their gold, silver, or diamonds come from and if they have an idea of their sources in general. Chances are the sales person will be prepared to answer, and maybe another client will hear your question and be intrigued.
- The same thing at supermarkets selling frozen shrimp; or when you buy shoes or a bag: Where does the leather come from? Or a T-shirt: Where was the cotton farmed?
- Ask someone who looks too young to work: Do you go to school? Are you getting paid for your job?
- Take your dog to the park and ask the nannies a few questions, or go to McDonald's on a Sunday and speak to the domestic workers: they will know who is not allowed to leave the house.
- When you tip the man who washed your car or the woman who did your nails, give it to them directly—don't put it in the tip box.
- Do the same with the maid or the waitress in a hotel: give the tip directly to her. So many jobs are outsourced in hotels, and you don't know if the worker is actually paid, or if someone else is paid for her work and doesn't redistribute it.

WRITE LETTERS AND E-MAILS

- Ask the police or your local authority if you can safely use the car washes, nail bars, or massage parlors in your neighborhood. Are they legitimate? Do they pay taxes?
- And more importantly: Can the police assure you that there is no slavery occurring there? If they receive twenty letters a month, they will have to answer and, believe me, they will check before answering.
- Write to your representative or senator to ask the same questions. Also ask what they are doing to make sure there is no forced labor in their constituency.

- Write to CEOs and ask them the same about their production lines or supply chains. If a CEO receives twenty of these letters a month, they cannot ignore them. Imagine if they received 2,000!

MAKE PHONE CALLS

- Call the human-trafficking helpline in your country or the police when you see something suspicious—for example, a woman who leaves the house only once a day to throw out the trash, and always looks afraid, or a child who washes dishes in the house across from you at 1 a.m. These two examples have actually led to arrests. People called the police with these tips, and the victims were rescued.
- Call the teacher, the director, or social services if you notice something abnormal at school, like a young girl who is very tired every morning. Make your children aware before they become teenagers.
- Speak to the police when you hear suspicious conversations in a café or a bar. Try to discreetly take a picture of the suspicious persons.

WORK PRO BONO

- Offer your services to a survivor for free if you are a lawyer, a psychotherapist, a yoga teacher.
- Give a survivor training if you know coding or another marketable skill. A number of NGOs can help you find survivors in desperate need of such help. And our foundation can certainly point you to a few.

DONATE

- Give money to the many charities and NGOs doing effective anti-trafficking work on the front lines. I know it can be difficult to figure out which ones are truly making a difference. We have just launched the Stop Slavery Hub where you will find this kind of information as well as news on trafficking worldwide.

If we each did these simple things, it would really start to make a difference toward securing freedom and justice for enslaved people.

What we need is a real acceleration in public awareness. In fact, it has already begun, thanks to many different factors—and the media.

MORE MEDIA INVESTIGATIONS

Media coverage has already increased enormously. In London, for instance, the *Evening Standard* carried out a three-month campaign in 2017 to speak of "The Slaves on Our Streets," covering every possible angle of this complex crime.

Investigative journalism has played a crucial role, and the Thomson Reuters Foundation is just one of the outlets that covers the issue on a daily basis on trust.org. It has really helped spread awareness because our articles are disseminated by Reuters wires and published every day by many different media outlets around the world. We now have journalists in India, Bangladesh, Thailand, Cambodia, Mexico, Brazil, the United Kingdom, and the United States covering the issue on a daily basis.

In India, radio has also begun to play a part: a popular New Delhi radio host has been discussing the fact that many domestic workers are trafficked and that in some cases their employers may not even know that the girls working in their kitchens have been reported missing by their parents. Radio is good for educating listeners on how to identify and avoid trafficking situations.

And radio is obviously the perfect medium for survivors to tell their stories, because they can be anonymous, while giving listeners an immediate sense of connection. More countries and communities could take their cue from these efforts to inform the public about the danger and prevalence of slavery, so that slavery becomes socially unacceptable.

These and many other media initiatives are promising, and we need much more coverage of this nature.

MORE LEGISLATION AND GOVERNMENT FUNDING

It's impossible to overstate the importance of putting the rule of law behind human rights. And for this reason, I am going to reiterate some points I have addressed in the last couple of chapters. Emma Bonino, the former foreign minister of Italy and a formidable activist, once told me that when she was campaigning for the right to abortion and for re-productive rights in the very Catholic Italy of the 1960s and 1970s, she was almost regarded as a prostitute. But when the law finally passed, she was suddenly accorded respect and welcomed into the mainstream.

When you think of it, exactly the same has happened with gay rights and same-sex marriage. So goes the dance between institutional change and social change.

Indeed, we should all take heart from the actions governments have already begun to take, following the lead of California and its Trans-parency in Supply Chains Act. In 2015, as I mentioned earlier, the United Kingdom followed with its Modern Slavery Act—one positive we can put to the credit of Theresa May—followed by France, Canada, the Netherlands, and Australia. In 2016, the Bali Process—made up of forty-five countries—issued a Declaration on People Smuggling and Trafficking in Persons, which underlines the role business must play.

The Philippines is a very interesting case, and while it still has many thousands of trafficking victims, I have great hope for the situation in that country, in large part because of a single NGO that has taken a very creative approach to fighting slavery and finally secured govern-ment support—before Rodrigo Duterte's election to office. In addition to staging interventions to rescue groups of trafficked children before they're sold; educating vulnerable people; and providing safety, shelter, and other critical support for victims, the Visayan Forum Foundation led by the sensational Cecilia Flores-Oebanda worked for decades to help pass and enforce the Philippines anti-trafficking law.

The first version was voted on in 2003, but after frustrations over its inefficacy, it was retooled and rebooted in 2012. Government ministers and the vice president of the Philippines himself credited the Visayan Forum with playing a central role in the shaping and implementation of this legislation.

The Philippines also has the most advanced law to protect domestic workers in Asia, and I am proud to have played a part in that just by putting Cecilia Flores-Oebanda in touch with the law firm White & Case through our TrustLaw program. The firm provided comparative legal research on legislation regarding domestic workers in different countries, which Cecilia used to inform legislators what would be the best practices for the Philippines. And a law on domestic workers was enacted, which has changed the life of two million workers in the country. In recent years, the number of trafficking prosecutions has skyrocketed in the Philippines. Likewise, the number of successful rescue operations was on the rise, thanks to a task force made up of Visayan and other NGOs working with government bodies.

In the United States, in spite of considerable effort by the Silicon Valley tech giants to repeal it—Google led the charge—a law was passed in March 2018 that finally allows prosecutors to hold websites such as Backpage.com liable for publishing information that enables sex trafficking. The new law allows victims to seek justice against their online traffickers. This is a major victory for the many brave survivors and NGOs who have been fighting for this legislation for years.

In April 2018, Backpage.com was seized in a joint move by several U.S. agencies, and the site is no longer operational. A few days later, authorities charged two of the site's founders and five employees with facilitating prostitution, pimping, and money laundering, among other things. Craigslist, Reddit, and other sites quickly announced that they would stop putting up sex ads.

I should note that the closure of Backpage.com stirred up a big debate in the United States with some voluntary sex workers arguing that to be unable to recruit customers online makes their work much more dangerous and difficult. This can indeed create some problems for legitimate sex workers, but for traffickers it is a significant issue, which is always a good thing.

The sad reality, though, is that as soon as these advertisements were barred from Backpage.com, dozens of other websites offered their services and brought the ads back. Traffickers move much faster than law enforcement.

As U.K. and U.S. law enforcement agencies and judiciaries begin to educate their people about identifying and responding to human trafficking, prosecutions are also increasing, with more in 2017 and 2018 than ever before. The number is still extremely small—in the thousands worldwide—but it's moving in the right direction.

However, governments around the world still spend only a pittance to fight slavery: not even one billion dollars a year—all countries combined—against a business of $150 billion. We must do better, and I'm sure we will in the very near future. The creation in 2017 of the Global Fund to End Modern Slavery, led by the formidable Jean Baderschneider and funded initially by the U.S. and U.K. governments, is a step in the right direction.

GROWING CROSS-SECTOR ENGAGEMENT

Corporations are starting to take notice at the same time as some anti-slavery NGOs gain funding and stature. Crucially, we are seeing a rise in public-private partnership and cooperation, the key to triggering real change on the ground. Progress cannot happen if we remain disconnected and without a coordinated approach across sectors.

At the Thomson Reuters Foundation, we approach the issue holistically, through TrustLaw, our pro bono program that helps the best NGOs on the front lines by taking over their legal needs for free; through our journalism with a team of reporters dedicated to covering modern slavery; through the Stop Slavery Award; through our annual Trust Conference. It is when we leverage all of one another's skills, when we work together in synch and not in silos, that progress occurs.

Slavery is no longer discussed in small groups behind closed doors. It is starting to take center stage, encouraging a worldwide conversation that will usher in a new era of awareness and action.

GATHERING MORE PRECISE DATA—AND SHARING IT

In one key area—data—the fight against slavery still lags far behind where it should be.

Data is the holy grail of the anti-trafficking world. Data collection and analysis is becoming a crucial tool in the pursuit of many trafficking cases. Law enforcement can analyze all sorts of information and images to root out traffickers. Trafficking frequently crosses borders and seas, and we've seen how prosecutors struggle when they have to rely solely on victims who may be scared to talk to the authorities because their ex-traffickers have threatened them.

In 2014, the Defense Advanced Research Projects Agency (DARPA), part of the U.S. Department of Defense, launched the Memex program to enable comprehensive new ways to search the whole web and find patterns. It was the brainchild of an ingenious young man named Chris White, who chose sex trafficking for his first, big, test project. The program helps law enforcement officers and others hunt down traffickers by understanding the profile of human trafficking on both the open web and the dark web.

The enormous volume of online sex sales would be impossible to tackle with conventional methods and commercial search engines. With Memex, one can look at a cluster of ads with common attributes—photos of the women and of their websites, physical addresses, and phone numbers—in order to find connections between different posts and different spaces online. One can use indicators such as code words, images, or branding tattoos to determine if someone is being trafficked.

As of fall 2017, 300 agencies were using Memex to find human-trafficking cases. Memex is no longer with DARPA but with Cyrus Vance's foundation, and his office uses it with success. The program has led to hundreds of arrests and convictions by a variety of law enforcement agencies in the United States, the United Kingdom, and France.

But Memex is not the only tool for collecting data related to slavery. Microsoft is doing its part to chase sex trafficking online and forced labor in supply chains. They cooperate with law enforcement on cybercrime, looking at sites such as Bing, Skype, and Telegram to determine how people search for child sex. Thorn, an anti-trafficking foundation in the United States created by Ashton Kutcher and Demi Moore, has developed various programs for analyzing seized images of child sex abuse and identifying and locating victims. Interpol uses similar victim-identification technology that is linked to law enforcement agencies and hotlines for reporting abuses in dozens of countries.

All these programs have enabled the identification of many thousands of child sex-trafficking victims. When identifying the victims leads to finding them, 90 percent of the time that also means finding the perpetrators. In most cases, they are within the close family.

As these kinds of technologies develop and expand, they will hopefully begin to outpace the traffickers and other predators.

I want to say a word here about "sextortion," which doesn't fit the exact definition of sex trafficking, but has become a huge danger to teenagers in the United States and is now spreading around the world.

Sextortion is when sexual favors are requested by a person in a position of authority in exchange for a service that should be free—at work or elsewhere. It's a form of corruption, except that instead of money, a more intimate service is sought. Its online form has become a way for adults to ask teenagers—boys and girls—to send increasingly explicit photos or videos of themselves. It starts as a game, or as flirting, and quickly turns into threats of publishing the photos on Facebook or other social media if the victims don't send more. It terrorizes the targeted teenagers and has led to a number of suicides.

The Thomson Reuters Foundation's TrustLaw program has organized legal research on the phenomenon with a view to transforming the law, and many U.S. states have recently changed their laws to make sextortion a crime that can be prosecuted.

The most famous recent victim of an attempt at sextortion is Jeff Bezos, the CEO of Amazon, who said he was being blackmailed by the *National Enquirer* with the threat of publishing sexually explicit photos if he didn't stop investigating the tabloid's reporting on him. "If in my position I can't stand up to this kind of extortion, how many people can?" Bezos wrote in February 2019.

Another reason to gather more and better data is to improve our knowledge of how many slaves there are in the world, until one day we will have an accurate figure. This will finally allow us to understand if this number is growing or diminishing and will greatly facilitate analysis and coordinated anti-trafficking efforts.

It is largely accepted that among the 40.3 million slaves in the world (ILO number) 70 percent are in forced labor and 30 percent in sex trafficking. But we also know that these percentages vary greatly from country to country: In India, for instance, experts believe it's closer to 85 percent forced labor and 15 percent sex trafficking, whereas in Southeast Asia, they think it is roughly 50/50. The data provided by Polaris, the U.S. helpline, already gives us a better grasp of what happens and in which U.S. states. In the United Kingdom, the official number of 13,000 enslaved people is largely underestimated, according to the Anti-Slavery Commissioner Kevin Hyland, and new figures from the Walk Free Foundation put it at 130,000.

The best description of the situation as we know it today came from Kevin Bales at the last Trust Conference: "If slavery were a state, it would have the population of Algeria, the GDP of Bulgaria, and be the third largest emitter of CO_2 in the world (because of slave-based deforestation in the Amazon)."

Bales has continued to pioneer far-ranging research on slavery at the University of Nottingham, and its Rights Lab has recently received £10 million in funding. He and his team are dedicated to improving data collection and are even beginning to crowdsource it. For example, brick kilns in India, Nepal, and Pakistan, which rely heavily on slave labor, can be seen in photos taken from space. We've never known how many brick kilns there are, or precisely where they are located. Now, individuals can help find them in satellite imagery.

Slavery was previously relegated to the world of anecdote. It is now moving into the more serious world of data and fact.

Measuring slavery is just one aspect of the interdisciplinary research conducted at Bales's Rights Lab, by the way: it has fourteen areas of focus within human trafficking, from the impact of migration to the consequences of environmental disasters. The team deploys its research for real-world solutions, sharing information and undertaking projects with NGOs, national and local governments, and corporations.

THE BANKS ALLIANCES

There is another effective way to harness the power of computers in this fight: following the money. Barry Koch was part of the financial intelligence unit at JPMorgan Chase in 2010 when the bank decided to see if it could investigate human trafficking. He conceived of the brilliant idea of looking into the "huge data pool" available to big banks, where one has the ability to analyze lots of "interesting things" in hundreds of millions of transactions every day. Looking at the credit card data of its clients, his department built financial models to identify the various characteristics of customers, transactions, and accounts that pointed to trafficking.

"We did quantitative analysis of accounts to look at how long they'd been open, or whether there were indicators of identity theft, or financial crimes," Koch told me. "We looked at business accounts to see if the activity was consistent with harboring a lot of people in the basement, or if it consisted of taking control of their assets: everybody cashing the payroll on the same day, everybody being paid exactly the same amount, no expenses. And we found through the alerts generated by the machine that those red flags we'd identified had a very high statistical correlation to likely trafficking rings."

One of Barry Koch's best stories is about a New York nail salon chain. Looking at its credit card data, he noticed that many clients were paying the shops between 11 p.m. and 5 a.m.—a pretty unusual time to get your nails done—and they never paid less than $100, which is expensive for a manicure. He shared the data with law enforcement, which investigated and dismantled the sex-trafficking ring.

After some of these busts, Barry and his team had the chance to ask the survivors if they knew how the traffickers opened their accounts, what days of the week they preferred, which products and services they used and which they avoided. Almost any kind of data might prove useful: zip codes, visa types, citizenship status, and so on. This human side of data collection has proven invaluable.

Barry told us about his work at our first conference in 2012, and I was so impressed by his techniques that I wanted to convince all the other banks to analyze data in the same way. Together, Barry and I organized the Banks Alliance against Trafficking in 2013, and I asked Cyrus Vance to co-host the working group with me because his authority and his track record in fighting sex trafficking were impressive. It worked so well that our foundation then organized something similar with European banks and, in 2019, with Asian banks.

The alliances bring together leading financial institutions, expert anti-trafficking NGOs, and law enforcement agencies to map the financial footprint of human trafficking in each country and track potential traffickers.

In 2014, we published the first set of red flags that the biggest U.S. banks had agreed to incorporate into their software in order to find suspicious information, which they would then share with law enforcement. FinCEN, the Financial Crimes Enforcement Network in the United States, adopted this tool, leading to a serious increase in banks reporting trafficking-related suspicious activity. In 2017, our European Alliance published the Anti-Trafficking Toolkit for Banks, which has since been endorsed by many governmental and financial institutions, as well as the Wolfberg Group, comprised of the fifteen biggest banks in the world. And in 2019, we launched the Asian toolkit.

Thankfully, the sharing of data to track human trafficking is becoming an industry best practice.

So how exactly do the banks do it?

They use software that generates alerts when it has created enough possible indicators of human trafficking, which can be anything from a lot of payments coming from a "geographic risk area of interest"—that is, a certain country or region known to have a high level of trafficking—to the regular use of "anonymous monetary instruments" like gift cards, to multiple cash deposits into a single account on the same day. The banks' investigators also pay attention to media reports of human trafficking. Furthermore, they rely on a lot of assistance and information from various anti-slavery NGOs, which have been fantastically helpful since Barry and I first conceived the alliance idea.

And of course, the financial institutions work closely with law enforcement on this issue. In one case, law enforcement asked the financial institutions to look into the records of an auto body shop, and sure enough they found an assortment of indicators, including "transactional activity inconsistent with the alleged business or expected activity," in the language used by the banks. In this case, the company credit card was used to purchase a lot of airline tickets, women's clothing, and toiletries; and the flights were purchased for third-party passengers, most of them female.

In another case, the bank's own monitoring system generated an alert for a checking account held by a Russian living in Miami because he was receiving payments "from an unknown source in Russia in a structured manner." Not only is Russia considered a geographic risk area of interest, but the payments exceeded the account holder's reported annual income. Again, the account showed many travel-related purchases, like airfare, hotels, and Airbnb.

In these ways, financial institutions have begun to play an absolutely crucial role in investigating traffickers and bringing them to justice. And the collaboration they have started to develop with law enforcement is crucial.

SUPPRESS THE KAFALA SYSTEM

There is one possible solution that would drastically reduce the number of slaves in the world: ending the Kafala system in the Gulf region and in Saudi Arabia, Lebanon, and Jordan. As I explained in an earlier chapter, the Kafala is a system of sponsorship that puts migrant workers at the total mercy of their employers for everything from their visas to their exit permits. Remember what happened to Deependra.

One country has started to show an interest in improving conditions for workers: Qatar, which has around two million migrant workers at any given time. Because Qatar is hosting the Football World Cup in 2022 and has started a massive infrastructure program, the country began to receive a lot of scrutiny and negative interest from the media. So the Qatar government decided to take action. In 2017, it moved its Committee for Combating Human Trafficking up to the ministerial level—quite a big statement. Then it announced a number of measures, such as limiting the working day to ten hours or forbidding companies to withhold exit visas from workers, and they established a minimum wage.

These are all revolutionary measures for the Gulf countries, measures that could simply explode the Kafala system in Qatar if implemented thoroughly. Although they have yet to be effectively implemented, this is obviously a step in the right direction and one that Saudi Arabia, Lebanon, the United Arab Emirates, and the rest would be wise to follow.

The fact that Qatar has decided to act on the issue, rather than resorting to meaningless public relations statements as they used to do, fills me with hope. It could change the lives of millions of people who, like Deependra, have been trapped in a system that keeps them in debt bondage even after they escape from hell.

PROVIDE SURVIVORS WITH MENTAL HEALTH TREATMENT

As we saw with Jennifer and Marcela, the psychological recovery of survivors is another aspect of human trafficking that has not been addressed properly. Survivors' mental health is crucial, and fundamental, to recovery. Without treatment, victims continue to suffer from PTSD and are often unable to move on with their lives, leaving them at risk of falling back into slavery.

And yet, with a few exceptions, existing treatment programs are insufficient. They are neither easily accessible nor affordable, they are far too short, and there are few professionals with adequate training.

For years now, I have been trying to create a group of psychologists and psychiatrists that could address the problem on a pro bono basis—

that is, at no cost for the survivor. The network is starting to take shape, with mental health professionals on both sides of the Atlantic ready to participate. But we need now to find the funding to create a stable program.

BUILD A SURVIVORS' ALLIANCE

In a similar kind of holistic approach, Survivor's Ink has one idea for bringing groups together: in every country, a national survivors' alliance that draws on the collective knowledge and connections of a solid network of survivor-led NGOs to provide victims with "wrapped-around services." For instance, this would mean that from the moment an NGO receives a call about a victim—maybe it is a girl, being released from rehab or jail, with nowhere to go—no matter where in the country the girl happened to be, the network could offer support and services: shelter, protection, legal assistance, job training, housing, and so on, to make sure that she doesn't fall back into the hands of her traffickers.

Their idea speaks directly to one of the biggest challenges of supporting survivors: providing them with long-term help on the lifelong road of sustained recovery.

MORE EDUCATION AND TRAINING

By education, I am not just referring to school. At school, children certainly should be made aware of their rights, of the dangers of modern slavery, of grooming techniques, and of the potential risks of taking loans.

But in addition to that, police forces all around the world should be trained to recognize signs of human trafficking. Likewise, social workers should not ignore basic signs that something is wrong. Judges and prosecutors should be educated on the issue and start implementing the applicable laws. All government employees, from diplomats to teachers to prison guards, need to be equipped with understanding and information, so that they know human trafficking when they see it and respond effectively.

Within government, the work has barely begun, and only in a few countries. And we know now that the best educators on the issue are the survivors themselves. At Trust Conference, I always start the first day with survivors speaking of their experience: The 600 delegates in the room immediately know why they are sitting there!

HELP THE BRAVE NONGOVERNMENTAL ORGANIZATIONS ON THE FRONT LINES

With so many dedicated NGOs, large and small, doing fantastic work all over the world, it's difficult for me to single out any for recognition. Here is just one example: Truckers Against Trafficking. It is a brilliant and simple idea that has made truck drivers in the United States alert to sex trafficking.

Kendis Paris realized one day that truck drivers very often find themselves in places where sex traffickers sell or exchange their victims: truck stops, rest areas, hotels, motels, city streets, loading docks. And she knew that at any given time, there are more truck drivers out on the roads and highways than there are police officers. She asked herself, "What if they understood the backstories behind the smiles and knock they get on their doors? What if a cultural shift took place, from, 'She's just a prostitute,' to, 'She may be a victim.'"

She created Truckers Against Trafficking (TAT) and trained drivers as first responders, to identify and report human trafficking. Drivers loved the idea and have helped hundreds of victims through thousands of calls to the national hotline when they have noticed something suspicious. Paris is expanding now into other countries and she encourages companies that transport products to have their drivers trained by TAT. Many groups, like Walmart, have trained their drivers, who are happy to feel useful.

We truly need a global shift in mind-set, of the kind that happened with smoking in the office or drunk driving, as Niall Ferguson said brilliantly, speaking of another issue. This worldwide shift will come from all of us, as consumers and citizens, refusing to participate in societies and economies that don't care about slavery. Enough is enough. And this, I hope, will come sooner rather than later.

11

My Heroes

Courage is resistance to fear, mastery of fear, not absence of fear.

—Mark Twain

I've told you the full stories of three extraordinary survivors: Jennifer Kempton, Marcela Loiaza, and Deependra Giri. They, together with other people featured in the book, such as Kailash Satyarthi, are my heroes.

But there are countless other survivors doing heroic work, including many who haven't ever recovered psychologically. For a few strong individuals who not only survive but also thrive after escaping slavery, there are millions of others who still suffer immensely and will never be able to fully repair the damage caused by years of enslavement. They are all in my thoughts and guiding my efforts.

But here I want to shine light on a few more who have also become my heroes during these last ten years.

NADIA MURAD, THE UNEXPECTED LEADER

In my realm, Nadia Murad would probably be the queen of the survivors.

All the sadness of the world is in her eyes, to a point that it is almost intimidating, and she looks at you with such gravity and intensity that her pain is palpable. Her will is astonishing; you feel nothing could stop this very brave woman. She commands immediate respect and although she is very young and petite, you can instantly see the leader in her.

Kidnapped, trafficked, and sold into slavery by Daesh—better known under the name they wanted to establish: Islamic State—Nadia was, at twenty-one, one of the thousands of Yazidi women and girls whose life was shattered the day the barbaric troops took control of the town of Sinjar and surrounding villages in Iraqi Kurdistan. Her family had a farm in the village of Kocho.

This day, August 3, 2014, was the cruelest day one could imagine: The terrorists separated men, women, and children, then took the men outside and killed them on the spot. They also killed the older women. They kept the younger ones and the children to use as slaves. Nadia saw six of her brothers taken to their deaths, followed by her mother, who was sixty-one.

For Daesh, the small community of the Yazidis—one of the oldest religions on earth, dating back to ancient Mesopotamia—deserves to be exterminated because they are apostates, the worst form of infidel. Daesh doesn't consider Yazidis human beings.

They took 6,500 women and children to various cities. For Nadia, it was Mosul, where she and others were sold to any men who wanted them. The kidnappers took pictures of them to make a catalog so their men could choose and change women whenever they wanted. Nadia tried to escape but was quickly recaptured and gang raped until she fainted. A life of violence and humiliations of all kinds ensued.

Three months later, she was brave enough to escape again. She found shelter in a house in Mosul where they organized her escape via smugglers. The Yazidi community has never hesitated to pay smugglers to rescue and save their women.

Nadia then was sent to Germany as a refugee. I didn't yet know her, but our paths soon crossed because at the Trust Women Conference in London in November 2014—just after her escape—two representatives of the Yazidis spoke of the genocide that was then taking place.

Ten days later, I was at a dinner in New York and met the deputy U.S. Ambassador to the United Nations, Sarah Mendelson, who had heard about my conference and asked me to find a Yazidi woman ready to speak at the Security Council in New York—not an easy task because the tragedy was so recent and the trauma so acute.

But when I told Murad Ismael, who heads the NGO Yazda and had spoken at Trust Conference, that this was an extraordinary opportunity to shed light on the Yazidi genocide at the top level of the United Nations, he said he would try his best to locate someone. And he found that Nadia was ready to speak of her ordeal at the hands of Daesh.

That she agreed to address such an intimidating audience was in itself remarkable: she was a fragile twenty-one-year-old, just saved from the worst experience on earth. And there she was, on the sixteenth of December in New York: so small in her seat, face bare of makeup, telling her dramatic story simply, just as it happened, with no crying or self-pity. The tears were not in her eyes but in the eyes of the ambassadors in the room, who were so extremely moved that they applauded her when she finished.

This, also, is exceptional: clapping is not the usual practice at the U.N. Security Council.

Her photo was published worldwide. The Yazidis had found their champion. Nadia and Murad wrote to me a few days later saying Trust Women and the U.N. Security Council had changed the course of their lives. First, because he found funding for his organization at my conference, and most of all because Nadia, after the United Nations, became the voice of the martyrs. The Iraqi government even proposed her for the Nobel Peace Prize.

Two months later, I was in Iraq, speaking at the first Yazidi conference, and I saw for myself her impact: when I mentioned Nadia's name, cheers started, and when they learned I knew her, they all started asking questions about her. Visiting the camps in Suleimani was a heartbreaking experience: The Yazidis were separate from the other refugees and all these young girls who had lived through hell under Daesh were spending their days doing nothing and worrying about their sisters still in the hands of the butchers and about the fates of their families. Nadia was their ray of hope.

Since then, she has become a U.N. goodwill ambassador for human trafficking and has met the Pope and a number of heads of state. Her main mission is to urge the international community to recognize the Yazidi extermination as genocide and take action. She also wants justice, with the traffickers and criminals paying for their crimes.

As she says, "We received sympathy and solidarity all over the world, but what we really need is concrete action to get justice and allow our community to return to its homeland." Her young nephew, Malik, who was taken with her by Daesh, was indoctrinated and trained as a soldier. He recently had an opportunity to leave but he refused, saying, "Yazidis are infidels who should convert and join ISIS." He was thirteen when he said this.

Nadia has received powerful support from one of the world's most noted celebrities, Amal Clooney, the human rights lawyer married to actor George Clooney. Amal and a team of pro bono lawyers help Nadia and Yazda document the atrocities, collect evidence of genocide, and try to get cases prosecuted.

French President Emmanuel Macron has pledged to demine the Sinjar region. Daesh has infested the whole country with mines, making it impossible for the refugees to return to their homeland. Nadia dreams of going home.

She is a survivor and a leader who needs a lot more than empathy.

After I finished writing this book, she did indeed receive the Nobel Peace Prize in December 2018!

EVELYN CHUMBOW, THE WARRIOR

Evelyn was born in Douala in Cameroon and was trafficked at nine as a domestic slave to a family in Maryland. It was an uncle who sold her, promising she would have a better education in America, the land of opportunities. She finally escaped just before her eighteenth birthday.

Like Nadia, who argues that empathy is not enough, Evelyn believes survivors "don't need compassion, they need jobs" to be able to reconstruct their lives. Sadly, often people feel empathy for survivors but cannot see them as potential professionals because they think they are too damaged.

"Train me and I'll be as good as you," Evelyn told the audience at our Trust Women Conference in 2014 in London. She was so convincing that lawyers from one of the biggest law firms in the world, Baker McKenzie, offered her a traineeship at their office in Washington, DC. She has been thriving there for four years and is now a project assistant. She is also a fantastic advertising asset for the firm as she has become very well-known around the United States.

She owes it all to her charisma, her force of conviction, her kindness to others—but most of all, her very strong presence. You cannot intimidate her.

And it is remarkable that she recovered so well after years of beatings and being treated like dirt. For seven years, she had to sleep on the ground, was beaten nude in front of the two children in her care, and more often than not, was forced to remain standing all night without falling asleep as punishment when her master was displeased with her. Her master, a woman who had emigrated from Cameroon and made good money in the United States, continually told Evelyn that she was ugly, her skin was too dark, and she was stupid and could never be educated. She was not sent to school and was never allowed even a day off from her duties.

Many would have looked for revenge. Astoundingly, Evelyn didn't, although her case was investigated and in the end her slaver was sentenced to prison—where she remains. But Evelyn tells me, "The fact that she is imprisoned never made me feel good, because she has two kids and these kids have been my kids too for so long, and I don't want them to suffer." Evelyn is one of the very few survivors I know who has seen her tormentor convicted, but this doesn't fill her with any special satisfaction.

Her kindness reverberates in all she does. Today, she sits on the boards of Free the Slaves and the Human Trafficking Center—two excellent NGOs fighting modern slavery—and is on the U.S. Advisory Council on Human Trafficking created by President Obama. She advocates in schools and with law enforcement. She tries to organize jobs for survivors. She never stops advocating. And she works in a big law firm.

Interestingly, the day she escaped from slavery, she just walked to the nearest Catholic church, where she found a priest who listened kindly to her. Reverend Paul could not really make sense of what had happened to this girl but was attuned enough to accompany her to a Catholic charity in Washington, DC, where they quickly diagnosed a case of modern slavery. A woman named Melanie took care of Evelyn and remains her closest advisor and friend to this day. "I trusted her immediately and still trust her more than anyone else," says Evelyn. The fact that she kept her capacity to trust is also very rare among victims of trafficking, especially immediately after they escape.

Melanie, who is an attorney, organized the investigation of Evelyn's case both in Cameroon and in Maryland. Evelyn had a hard time with the FBI, who didn't believe her and thought she was just trying to get her green card. Eventually, her case came to trial and the slaver was sentenced to seventeen years in prison; she had been convicted earlier for embezzlement. She was also ordered to pay Evelyn $100,000 in compensation for her years of work for no wages. Of course, Evelyn never received that money.

One of Evelyn's remarkable contributions is reminding authorities and advocates in the United States that slavery is not confined to sex, but that the large majority of slaves are forced to work in families as unpaid domestics, in factories at all kind of jobs, in agriculture, or in the fashion industry.

She meets survivors of both kinds of slavery and says that when you put them in the same room to share experiences, you can find very little difference: They have the same sense of total betrayal, total helplessness, and trauma. The trauma is very similar. Especially because, very often, the people trapped in forced labor are also sexually abused and raped.

Evelyn visited Cameroon in 2012, sixteen years after she left, and saw her mother and father, who had heard no news of her since she left. She was so happy to meet them again, especially her father. After her return to the United States, she discovered that she was pregnant and married her boyfriend. Her little boy is today her reason to move forward in life. She is very ambitious, for herself and for him. Recently Evelyn's husband left her and she is once again in a very precarious situation because of the $60,000 loan she took to study.

But I know nothing will stop her.

SUNITA DANUWAR, THE NEPALESE MOTHER OF ALL

After the 2015 earthquake, Nepal became the poorest country in Asia, surpassing Afghanistan. Trafficking is an endemic sickness in this beautiful country, where people have to migrate to find work and send money home. It is estimated that one Nepalese in one hundred could be subject to some form of slavery today.

Sunita Danuwar was fourteen years old when she was taken and sold in the sinister red-light district of Mumbai. For five years, she was a sex slave, sold every day to thirty or more men in the filthiest brothel imaginable.

In 1996, she was freed when the Indian police raided a few brothels, releasing 500 girls, of which almost 200 were Nepalese. Young girls from Nepal are highly valued in India for their fairer skin and their beautiful smiles. This raid was widely publicized all over India and Nepal as a show of police effectiveness.

But their government refused to repatriate them, for fear that they would spread HIV/AIDS in the country. In the end, they were permitted to leave their squalid shelters in India—where they were still stigmatized as prostitutes—to return to Nepal, thanks to a few NGOs. And as soon as they were back in Nepal, they were all confined to a hospital in a special, separate unit to undergo HIV tests. Most of the women were found positive. Even the doctors treated them as pestiferous, as they didn't know at the time how to deal with the virus.

It took Sunita and her friends months before they realized that being trafficked and sold into prostitution was not their fault and that they were indeed victims of a crime. That was when they decided to create an NGO to help other survivors like them. But to be able to do so, they had to prove their Nepalese citizenship. The task wasn't an easy one: they had to go back to their villages and find their families—families they had left many years before as young children. They had to convince their fathers to recognize them, a difficult prospect when some were ashamed that their daughters had been prostitutes. They didn't understand that it was slavery, not prostitution. "Some of us had to bribe our own fathers," Sunita told me when I was in Nepal in 2016.

All in all, it took them four years until finally, in 2000, they were able to set up Shakti Samuha, thanks to a grant of 500,000 rupees (some $8,000) from Mama Cash, a brave international NGO. Sunita remains the president of Shakti Samuha to this day. They have four shelters in Nepal offering fantastic programs of rehabilitation, training, legal aid, and psychological support to hundreds of survivors whom the organization rescues every year.

As part of the rehabilitation program, a girl who has been rescued spends three months in intense psychological support. Anxiety and depression are constantly assessed, and a case manager prepares a recovery plan for each and every survivor. After three months, if the survivor wants to go back home, the organization determines if it is feasible or if there is too great a danger that she could be enslaved again.

A psychological recovery takes a minimum of six months—and these are the rare best cases; a slow recovery can take up to three years, during which victims receive different kinds of treatment and training. When they are strong enough, they are then moved to "halfway homes" where they can come and go freely for six to twelve months. If they find a job, they take an apartment of their own.

What Sunita and her friends have built in Nepal is truly remarkable. Today, these former child slaves receive support from many international donors, like the Freedom Fund, to help them rescue and rehabilitate victims. They also do prevention work in villages where so many parents still believe that sending their daughter to Kathmandu is the only option to secure good lives for them, away from acute poverty.

MARTINA VANDENBERG, THE LAWYER WHO GIVES A HELPING HAND

Martina Vandenberg is a very smart American lawyer who has dedicated her life to fighting human trafficking and particularly to helping victims of forced labor. "That's the secret of trafficking: Everybody comes for the sex and stays for the labor," she says with humor, quoting the anthropologist Juhu Thukral.

She will always go the extra mile to help a survivor, and her kindness and humanity are what people remember first about Martina. Thanks to her, modern-day slaves can sue their traffickers and win prosecutions more often than not—because Martina usually gets financial compensation to the survivor—even if the trafficker happens to be a diplomat hiding behind diplomatic immunity while enslaving a maid at his residence in Washington, DC.

Martina has travelled extensively, living in Russia and spending months in Israel and Bosnia for research, before and during her time at Human Rights Watch, one of the best human rights NGOs in the world. She then became an attorney specializing in complex commercial litigations for a big international firm, but she found her fulfilment in pro bono work, helping victims for free, as so many good lawyers do.

In 2012, she created the pro bono Human Trafficking Legal Center—thanks to the support of George Soros's Open Society Foundations—with the goal of providing each survivor with a lawyer to solve some of the many issues they face coming out of hell.

At the start, her legal center was a real one-woman show, but it has evolved now into an efficient organization that not only helps survivors with legal services but also publishes reports, collects data, and does quantitative assessments of what happens in U.S. courts. It is also a huge resource for finding documents, information, laws, and treaties on the issue of human trafficking worldwide.

I've known Martina since my first conference in 2012, where she and a few others, like David Batstone of Not for Sale, Kevin Bales of Free the Slaves, and Benjamin Skinner of Transparentem, helped me navigate the trafficking world. She lives in Washington, DC, and I live in London, but not a month goes by without our speaking about pressing issues. She has been so patient with me and my many questions and each year has moderated the survivors' panel, with an extraordinary attention to each of them. I could not have done what I started to do at the Trust Conference without her intelligence and her willingness to share.

At the first meeting of the Banks Alliance that I co-hosted with Cyrus Vance, the district attorney for New York, she said to all the biggest American banks represented around the table, "When I see you, I don't see money, I see data." She could not have done a better summary of what we were trying to launch: a system for having the banks look at the credit-card data of their clients to flag instances of human trafficking.

Martina was instrumental in the success of this working group and in helping my team write the principles of the alliance, a toolkit that was immediately adopted by FinCEN (Financial Crime Enforcement Network), the American clearinghouse for money laundering, and that has led to more traffickers being tried and convicted. She says that trafficking is very often "migration gone badly wrong": most modern slaves move voluntarily and cross borders, but then something goes wrong along the way and they end up in the hands of traffickers.

Survivors are lucky to find such a good lawyer: she takes their calls, advises them on finding jobs, and helps them through all their difficulties and circumstances.

I know that a lot of them will agree with me when I say she is a hero.

KEVIN BALES, THE PIONEER

Kevin Bales is an American academic interested in human rights who has done more to increase our knowledge of modern slavery than anybody. He discovered when in his thirties that slavery is not a relic from the past but a very modern issue, and he decided to investigate.

He travelled the world and met all kinds of slaves in Africa, France, the United States, and Asia, and has written ten books about slavery. My favorite is his first, *Disposable People*, published in 1999 and nominated for a Pulitzer.

Kevin has also attacked the problem of data and published the first Global Slavery Index with the Walk Free Foundation. The index forced the ILO (International Labor Organization) to revise their estimate dramatically upward in September 2017 from 20.9 million slaves in the world to 40.3 million. It's very helpful to have a number around which we all can rally—even if most specialists think the real number is much higher.

As Kevin noted last summer over breakfast at my place in Notting Hill, "The fight against slavery is progressing, but the number of slaves is not falling yet." Like me, he waits for the global shift in mind-set that will someday lead the world to refuse any form of slavery.

That morning I was talking to him about the network that I wanted to create to connect psychologists, psychiatrists, and practitioners with survivors whom they would help pro bono. He understands perfectly the needs to help address the problems of survivors' mental health and explains well "why it is so difficult for them to tell their stories straight, because the things get jumbled in their minds in terms of times sequences; it's so confused, it's part of their PTSD."

I told him how it was a discussion with a stunningly beautiful survivor that triggered in me the will to take action and fight human trafficking. Somaly Mam was at the Fortune's Most Powerful Women Conference in California in September 2011, and we sat together at dinner and spoke for three hours—in French.

She had been sold as a child in Cambodia and grew up in brothels before being rescued by a French man who was her client and who helped her build her foundation a few years later. She gave me her book and I read it in one go that very night.

A few years after, in 2014, she was accused of fabrication and organizing fake rescues of girls from brothels for a television program. She fell out of grace, after having been celebrated by many celebrities, politicians, and the media and after having raised millions for anti-trafficking efforts and the Somaly Mam Foundation. I felt so bad for her, but at the same time I was relieved that I had never invited her to speak at my conference—I don't know why, something didn't completely add up for me in the story she was telling and I thought she was becoming too much of a star for her own good. And yet, she was the one who really inspired my move into this field and my urgency to take action. My mixed feelings about her have remained to this day. But mixed feelings are the texture of human nature, no?

And Kevin—who sat for a while on the board of the Somaly Mam Foundation—told me, "The fact that she became an icon is part of her tragedy. Because one minute she is working in Cambodia and recovering with her husband's help, and then suddenly *Vogue* shoots her into the stratosphere! She was living in a reality that was hard enough, and then she is propelled into an unreality of fame and glamour with the whole New York buzz. I mean, I would hardly survive that."

I love Kevin for his humanity: he expressed in a few sentences what nobody dared to say publicly. Somaly Mam is not a bad woman, she was just not equipped for so much glamour and buzz—and so many requests from so many media who wanted to film her in action. Hers is a unique story, but it shows that even when survivors flourish, their scarring damages them in ways that are not always predictable. Kevin, in his assessment of Somaly, made this tragic fact instantly clear.

Today Kevin Bales is a happy man: he has a young wife and a five-year-old daughter and has just received £10 million from the U.K. government to do research on human trafficking. His lab at Nottingham University has fourteen lines of research, from data to mental health.

We have already learned a great deal from their work. For instance, it has analyzed one million words used by five slaves to tell their stories and has discovered that slaves almost never use the future tense, always the past or the present. As Kevin puts it, "Slaves live in an eternal forced present." The slaveholders don't want them to think of the future—or the past: too many risks there, they must think they have no future. "Slaves use 'me,' not 'I'; they think of themselves as an object, not a subject." His fascinating research shows how ignorant we remain.

Interestingly, Kevin says that even with so much awareness of modern slavery, he still has the greatest difficulty populating his lab with experts, because there are so few real specialists. That's why he takes some brilliant young scholars and helps them become great slavery experts—as he has done with so many people before.

ADITI WANCHOO, THE BUSINESS KNIGHT

Aditi Wanchoo is a very outgoing person who has a master's degree in psychology and got into the NGO world by volunteering with Greenpeace in Bombay, asking drivers at busy traffic lights to give funds for a cleaner world. A pretty tough job, but she shone at it: she had men signing up for twenty dollars a year and giving their credit card details to a girl they didn't even know!

Soon Greenpeace gave her a promotion and she did major donor fundraising at Greenpeace India. But after four years, she understood that to effect real social change, you would be better placed in a business, and possibly a big one, rather than in an advocacy group.

So she moved to Accenture, in their Corporate Social Responsibility Department in India, where she convinced the department head to give the 100,000 staff time to train disadvantaged youth in "skills to succeed," like coding and other technical competencies. She now works at Adidas in Hong Kong, where she leads their global Modern Slavery

Outreach Programme. Slavery was new to her three years ago when she joined, but she quickly discovered that this was her purpose in life: to stop the exploitation of workers and impose policies respecting human rights in countries where common practice is usually to violate them.

Adidas didn't wait for Aditi to look at how to make its supply chains transparent: they started twenty years ago and were among the pioneers. But she has certainly accelerated the company's good practices and expanded them to include its processing facilities and sources for raw materials.

She has learned a lot from her boss at Adidas, Bill Anderson, the vice president of Social & Environmental Affairs. One particularly important strategy he taught her: don't be shy about calling a cat, a cat. Their program has the word "slavery" in its name.

Quite a big statement if you think of it: if all corporations had a no-slavery policy, the world would be more alert to the issue than it is today. Adidas's anti-slavery practices start with recruitment: they have a zero recruitment fee policy for their staff of 1.3 million people.

Aditi and her team make sure that their suppliers adopt and implement the same policy. They train all suppliers in their best practices and make certain that they understand that they'd better implement these rules quickly or a chance audit will find them out sooner rather than later. Adidas has done this in all the "difficult" countries like Vietnam, Cambodia, Indonesia, China, and Taiwan—but also in Brazil and Argentina for leather and Turkey for cotton.

Adidas's website is full of information on where they buy their raw material and who their suppliers are. They even have a "human rights defenders' policy." I think only three global companies have one of those.

Adidas is also a company that gives full recognition to its staff: when Adidas received the Stop Slavery Award for being "The Outstanding Winner" above all the other corporations in 2017, they did not send the CEO to receive the Anish Kapoor statue in London. They sent Aditi Wanchoo, their anti-slavery champion.

At forty, she has plenty of time to grow, and I have no doubt she is just at the start of delivering big things in the fight to end slavery.

KEVIN HYLAND, THE INDEPENDENT COMMISSIONER

Kevin Hyland is a top policeman who was appointed Independent Anti-Slavery Commissioner just before the United Kingdom's Modern Slavery Act was put in place in 2015. He was the first official in the world to receive this title, and he fully deserved it after leading the anti-trafficking unit of the London Metropolitan Police with impact and integrity. He owes his appointment to the vision of the then–Home Secretary, Prime Minister Theresa May, who has exercised more leadership in the fight against slavery than at the helm of her country.

Kevin is an incredibly modest and trustworthy man who specialized in fighting organized crime and corruption, including police corruption in the United Kingdom, and was good at catching criminals. He is fearless and has always tried to think of issues from the victims' point of view. He never tries to hide the shortcomings of law enforcement or government agencies when it comes to modern slavery in the United Kingdom.

He sees himself as the voice of those individuals who have been enslaved and he wants to make sure that their lives will get better and safer. This victim-centric approach is rare enough to merit mention: there are not that many people in positions of power who want to give a voice to the voiceless and listen to them once they are rescued.

Kevin is so good at this that I asked him to be the moderator for the survivors' panel at our 2017 Trust Conference in London, where his humanity was in full view. He uses his new authority to push for more action and more coordination, at the risk of being unpopular in some power circles. He perfectly understands the crucial role media plays in raising awareness and all over England and Wales, he points out slavery in car washes and nail salons, businesses full of migrants who have been stripped of all their rights by violent traffickers.

The "anti-slavery tsar"—as the U.K. tabloids have nicknamed him—is a fervent Catholic and helped create the Santa Marta Group, made up of police chiefs and bishops around the world who come together to fight slavery. Pope Francis, who supports the Santa Marta Group, has brought the full weight of the Church to this fight, saying recently that he "never loses an occasion to denounce human trafficking as a crime against humanity." The Pope also encourages young people to watch for signs that someone might be living in slavery and to speak up and have the courage to say what they see happening around them.

Kevin Hyland thinks that "there are a lot more than 13,000 modern slaves in the United Kingdom and that all we know points to a much higher number, with people reduced to slavery in agriculture, in construction, as domestics, in car washes or nail salons, as well as sex slavery."

He was one of the influential voices asking that modern slavery be part of the Sustainable Development Goals for 2030, adopted by the United Nations. Goal 16 includes the eradication of modern slavery.

Kevin also clearly sees the role that business can play and is a great spokesperson for the annual declarations required of U.K. corporations, under the Modern Slavery Act, to explain what they are doing to clean their supply chains of forced labor. He is a very diligent member of my jury for the Stop Slavery Award, along with Kailash Satyarthi, John Ruggie, Cyrus Vance, Patricia Sellers (a judge at the International Court of Justice), and Ken Roth, head of Human Rights Watch.

Kevin Hyland stepped down from his job in the summer of 2018 out of frustration of not being able to deliver more and is now back in his native Ireland, still working on anti-slavery issues.

I could speak of many more individuals who are doing heroic work in difficult countries like Pakistan or Cambodia, Nigeria or Vietnam. Many come to the Trust Conference and we do our best to keep in touch and help them along the way. They are the reason I am so confident that one day, together, we will start to win the fight.

This is certainly not the beginning of the end, but as Churchill said during the dark days of World War II, it may be the end of the beginning.

Written between January 2017 and June 2018
London, Siena, Bellagio

Index

Note: The photo insert images are indexed as *p1, p2, p3,* etc.

Bonino, Emma, reproductive rights campaigning of, 152–53

C&A Foundation, 146
Chumbow, Evelyn, 23–24; advocacy work of, 170; Baker McKenzie traineeship of, 169; Cameroon visit of, 171; domestic slave trafficking of, 168; FBI hard time of, 170; master mistreatment of, 169; slavery escape of, 170; slavery survivors similarities and, 170–71; slavery types reminding of, 170; strong presence of, 169; survivor job needs of, 169; tormentor conviction feelings of, 169; trust capacity of, 170; Trust Conference appearance of, 169
Churchill, Winston, 180
CID. *See* Criminal Investigation Department
Clooney, Amal, 168
Clooney, George, 168
Committee for Combating Human Trafficking, Qatar, 162
compassion, 4, 31, 75, 85
consumer, informed, 142–43, 147, 149; anti-trafficking charities and NGO donation of, 151; CEO supply chain question of, 151; human-trafficking helpline or police suspicious call of, 151; jewelry shop sources question for, 150; letter and e-mail writing as, 150–51; nannies or domestic workers question for, 150; phone call making of, 151; police neighborhood questions of, 150; police no slavery questions

of, 150; questions asking of, 150; representative or senator forced labor question of, 150; school abnormal teacher call of, 151; supermarket or T-shirt question for, 150; survivor free service offer of, 151; survivor training given by, 151; suspicious conversations reporting of, 151; tip directly as, 150; young worker question for, 150
Criminal Investigation Department (CID), 135

Danuwar, Sunita: government refusal to repatriate, 171; hospital confinement and doctor treatment of, 171–72; Indian police raid freeing of, 171; international donors support of, 173; Nepalese citizenship proving of, 172; prevention work of, 173; prostitute stigmatization of, 171; psychological recovery program of, 172; rehabilitation program of, 172; sex slave trafficking of, 171; Shakti Samuha NGO creation of, 172; victim realization of, 172
DARPA. *See* Defense Advanced Research Projects Agency
death threats, 24, 51, 63
"debt bondage," xiv–xv, 30, 41, 140–41, 152; legal labor look of, 60; in Mauritania, 43–44; no rules in, 45; resource lack in proving, 62–63; in sex trafficking, 47; traditional and hereditary, 43
Declaration on People Smuggling and Trafficking in Persons, Bali Process, 153